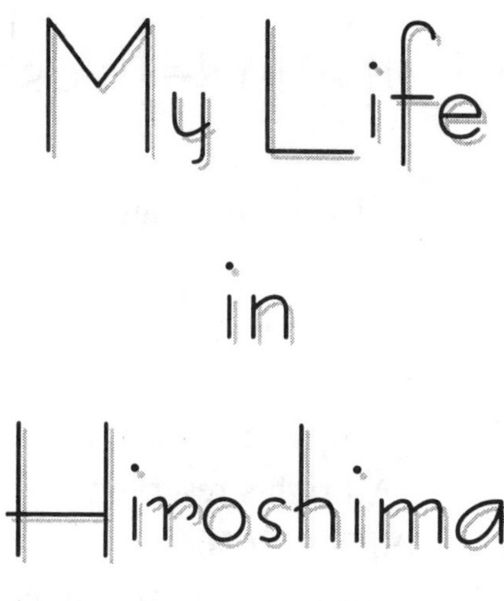

1952 - 1981

by

DORIS HARTMAN

Foreword by
FRANCES BRAY

Published by
Van Volumes
Three Rivers, Massachusetts

My Life in Hiroshima

Doris Hartman

Copyright, 2000

ISBN 0-9656620-5-5
Library of Congress Control Number: 00-132662

Address all correspondence to:
The Reverend Doris Hartman
216 Spencer Drive
Amherst, MA 01002

Published by:
Van Volumes
Three Rivers, Massachusetts

DEDICATION

To my colleagues and students of Hiroshima Jo Gakuin and the people of Furuichi who helped me to fulfill my calling, and who enriched my life. And also to my neighbor, Richard Kretschmann, without whose computer skills, I could not have produced this book.

--Doris Hartman

FOREWORD

We await with great anticipation the publication of the memoirs of Doris Hartman whom I have known for nearly 70 years. My Father was her pastor. Our lives have somewhat paralleled from our days in Epworth League to our service in Japan. I always admired her successful leadership in anything that she undertook. We weren't in close touch for awhile and so in 1952 we were delightfully surprised to arrive in Japan within a few months of each other. After teaching at Hiroshima Jo Gakuin, her pioneering spirit rose again and she moved into an all-Japanese community to help found a new church. Again I admired her courage to go it alone because I had my family with me. She was most successful in her ministerial work. There is significant spiritual uplift in reading this most interesting story of her life.

--Frances Hutchison Bray

TABLE OF CONTENTS

1. My Early Years

In my wildest fantasy I never thought I would some day think of Hiroshima, Japan, as my second hometown. Growing up in a small Midwestern town as a very shy and introverted child, I never dreamed I would some day become a minister preaching in another language. I had never known a woman minister except some spectacular evangelist like Aimee Semple McPherson. I certainly had no wish to become like her.

How did this Midwestern girl who always dreamed of being a high school English teacher end up as a missionary in this far off place? My journey began with my parents who left Cincinnati to make their home in a small Ohio town where there was a Christian college. They wanted their children to have the education that had been denied them. They wanted a change from their families which had little or no connections with church life.

My early life centered around the Methodist Church, but my Christian faith only became real to me during my high school and college years. During those formative years, we had a minister, the Rev. Clyde Hutchison, who was especially good at working with young people. For the first time in my memory we had a vital youth group. The minister's three older children served to attract many of us as well as his skilled leadership. It was during my junior high school years that the West family with their five children moved to our town and became members of our church. Two of the girls were about my age, and their two boys were near the ages of my younger brothers. These girls became my best friends and for the first time I had friends with whom I could share my hopes and dreams.

This combination of Wests, Hutchisons and Hartmans provided a core group for our Epworth League which met every Sunday evening. We formed the habit of having a get-together of our three families after we had been to Epworth League and the union church service on Sunday night, alternating meeting at the three homes. In addition to having fun, we tried to solve the problems of the world in our discussions. We called this the Sunday Night Club, and we formed such close bonds that we continued our friendship even after our paths scattered us across the world.

After graduation the minister's son, Clyde, married Jane West, linking those two families. In 1952, the minister's daughter, Frances and her husband, Bill Bray, then living in Oregon, applied to the mission board for service in Japan. Without my knowing about their plans, I applied that same year from Vermont. For the next 29 years we lived close enough to visit from time to time in Japan.

Thanks to our minister we took part in many church conferences and camps which enabled us to widen our horizons beyond our own church and our own denomination. He challenged us to raise funds to enable our whole group to rent a cottage at a Methodist youth camp for a week. For the first time I began to learn more about the world situation and what we could do about it. That was during the early thirties when many ministers were pacifists in reaction to World War 1. They were also proponents of the "social gospel" which emphasized putting into practice the radical teachings of Jesus. Many of us became pacifists, although we didn't know just what that would entail until war broke out again. As a child I was very shy, but Mr. Hutchison helped me to take leadership by persuading me to teach a Sunday school class, and to serve as president of our youth group. It was at his urging that I ventured to the interdenominational Camp Indianola sponsored by the Ohio Council of Churches even though I had to go alone. This was a leadership training course where excellent counselors helped give me more confidence by offering practical help in how to teach children. I even volunteered to help organize an interdenominational Vacation Bible School in our town after going back home though it had never been done before. Since we had all the churches from which to recruit teachers, we were able to have a capable staff, and it turned out to be successful. I continued going to that camp every summer during my college years.

I went to Cedarville College, the small Reformed Presbyterian school located just across the street from our house. I attended compulsory chapel every day, but I don't remember as much about the content of those talks as I do of our minister's practical sermons. The college had strict rules against smoking, drinking, and dancing on campus. But my church life helped me think about deeper social problems. I was strongly influenced by reading the life stories of Jane Addams of Hull House, Kagawa of Japan, and Muriel Lester of London. I wanted to do something to make society better. There were times when I believed God was calling me to some great work that would make a difference in the world.

Our college trained elementary teachers with a two year course and high school teachers with four years of liberal arts course. I had always dreamed of being a teacher as I enjoyed school and I did well in my studies. In those days, teaching was the model for women which I saw around me. We had an unusually gifted professor who headed the education department. He inspired me even more to believe that I could become an ideal teacher. Although I would like to have gone to a larger college away from home which seemed more exciting, I realized later that I was lucky to have that professor who had a real genius for inspiring us to want to be good teachers.

During the closing worship of our summer church camps, we were challenged to commit our lives to what was called full-time Christian work which meant the ministry or missionary service. But Mr. Hutchison often said we could serve God in ordinary vocations as well. When graduation time came, I followed in the footsteps of most of our student body by looking for a teaching job. Since I graduated in the depth of the great depression, teachers were a dime a dozen. Wherever I went to be interviewed, I found a line of twenty or more people applying for the job. School boards preferred those with experience. So it was quite a shock when I received word from a very small high school in Highland County telling me I had been chosen to teach English and Latin. I found out later there had been some kind of community dispute which resulted in a whole new school board. So perhaps they didn't know any better than to hire such a young (I was not quite 21) inexperienced teacher. I also learned there were few applicants with a Latin major.

I looked forward to becoming an ideal teacher whom the students would love and admire. I wanted to be someone who understood and responded to their feelings. I believed I could serve God in this profession as well as in specific church work. I had high hopes of making my classes so interesting that everyone would enjoy learning. I found the reality very different. Trying to teach large classes of restless junior high boys who longed to be out hunting and fishing took skills I had not yet developed. I enjoyed my small Latin and English classes in the senior high, but the junior high kids were too much for me. After two years, the high school had to merge with a nearby school as we had fewer than 100 pupils.

I managed to find another job in my home county at a large centralized high school in a rural area. I still had some discipline problems, though there were many students whom I enjoyed teaching. I stuck it out for three years, but then I decided to resign and begin a new career. I agonized about this decision, but I felt sure I could find some work where God could use my talents in a more productive way. During those enjoyable summer camp sessions at Indianola, I had discovered there was such a job as director of religious education in some larger churches. By that time I was enjoying my extra-curricular church responsibilities more than the work for which I was getting paid. Two of my Sunday Night Club friends had enrolled in a religious education course in Oberlin. When I visited them, the professors helped me to research various seminaries to find one which fit my needs.

So at the age of 26, I enrolled in the School of Religious Education in Hartford Seminary Foundation in Hartford, Connecticut, to study for a Masters' degree. I thoroughly enjoyed those two years full of challenge and new experiences. I felt I was able to take advantage of the classes more than those who had come directly from college. Since I knew my weak points, I was eager to learn how to overcome them. I came under the influence of an unusually gifted teacher, Edna Baxter, who gave me valuable guidance. She helped me gain self confidence as she supervised my field work in a church youth group.

A few young women were studying in the School of Theology to become ministers. I wondered why they didn't stick to being religious education directors which seemed to me a more appropriate vocation for women. It never occurred to me that I would ever become a minister. For the first time I came to know students from India, China, Japan, and Europe. Another new and exciting experience was meeting missionaries from various parts of the world who came to our School of Missions, one of the three schools in the Foundation. I looked up to those missionaries, but I didn't feel I had a special call to the mission field at that time. I had applied for the position as a director of Christian education in several large churches. But by the time of graduation I had no offer. I volunteered to spend the summer in a depressed area of Vermont in *The Summer Projects* sponsored by the Vermont Church Council of Churches. That was when I met and worked with the Rev. Myra Borden, who became my role model of a woman minister. After serving in several rural churches, she had created this summer work where she recruited college and seminary students to go in pairs to isolated areas where there were churches without pastors. We spent a week calling in the homes where there were young children. We invited them to a two-week vacation Bible school at the church. We recruited lay people for transportation. We found nearby ministers to lead Sunday services. We held recreation events for young people. Myra Borden did a thorough job of providing training for us at a Methodist related college before we went to our assignments. We each received a detailed manual with daily lesson plans, games, and crafts.

I found it rewarding to work with children who eagerly absorbed what we had to offer. I fell in love with Vermont with its beautiful lakes and mountains, a contrast to the flat lands of Ohio.

Myra Borden had persuaded a philanthropic business executive, Mr. Turrell, who summered in Vermont, to help children in the rural slums of Vermont in the same way he contributed to needy children in New York City slums. Eventually she convinced him that if the Council could hire another staff person to do Christian education in the churches, she would be free to work with needy children in isolated areas all year instead of just during the summer months. When the Vermont Church Council offered me that new job, I was delighted. I had hoped to work in rural churches, but I knew that large city churches were usually the ones which could afford to hire a director of Christian education.

From the very beginning, I loved the work in Vermont. Making my headquarters in Burlington, I traveled around the state to many small churches where I set up week-end church school clinics. My goal was to encourage teachers to use new and more creative methods in their church schools. Often I spoke in those churches to help the members realize the importance of having a good program for their children and young people. I felt that I had really found a way to use my various talents in serving God.

The executive secretary of the Vermont Church Council, Rev. Hugh Williams, had told me that Mr. Turrell had agreed to subsidize this new position as a pilot project for six months. He explained that Mr. Turrell always worked that way, but he was quite sure he would want to continue it beyond that deadline. So it came as a great shock when he told me Mr. Turrell would not continue the subsidy beyond February. He assured me that the Council was pleased with my work, but when Mr. Turrell read my monthly reports, he saw that I was working with church school teachers more than with children. He had a strong feeling that the money from the Turrell Foundation should go for work directly with children. Even though Mr. Williams tried to show him this work was indirectly contributing toward children's well-being, he could not be persuaded. So there I was in the middle of a Vermont winter a thousand miles from home without a job.

2. How I Became A Missionary

I was only temporarily without a job. Mr. Williams was determined to find a way for me to continue working in Vermont. Although he knew the Council did not have the budget for my staff job, he realized there were rural areas where I could work with children, if I would take the pastorate of a small church. That would convince Mr. Turrell to continue the subsidy. As I was very eager to stay in Vermont, I agreed to such a possibility.

A small Union Church (Congregational and Methodist) in Waterville, was hoping to find a part time pastor. For several years they had an elderly retired minister from a nearby town who came only on Sundays. During the previous summer they had enjoyed the services of a young seminarian who had come to live in the village. He gave inspiring sermons, started a junior choir, took young people to camp, and gave new life to the church. They didn't want to go back to their elderly pastor. They had asked the Council to recommend supply pastors each Sunday. I agreed to preach at the church onc Sunday with the understanding that I would consider taking the pastorate if they offered it to me.

Although I had spoken in churches about Christian education, I had never really preached a sermon before. I spent many hours in my study preparing for that first sermon. I am sure I dumped my whole theological knowledge on them. But they liked me well enough to ask me to return the following Sunday. That meant I had to come up with still another sermon, which was a major task! After the second sermon, they asked me to serve as their pastor. They took me to a nearby family where I could have a small upstairs suite for my bedroom and study. Emma Davis, the daughter of one of the church members, and her husband Kenneth, lived there. Some years earlier they had become members of the Nazarene Church which had broken off from the Union Church about thirty years previously.

This was a difficult decision to make. After enjoying cooperative living with three young career women in the delightful city of Burlington with its beautiful sunsets over Lake Champlain, I wondered how well I could adjust to living in that small village. It was separated from any paved road by about six miles. It would mean adjusting to living with a family instead of having an independent life style. There was a real challenge, however, in taking on such a church. Could I help bring new life to the congregation? Could I find enough schools where I could teach the Bible to children? Would that fulfill the requirement of working directly with children that would guarantee a continuation of my Turrell Foundation subsidy? After I agreed to take this leap of faith, I had to inform the District Superintendent of the Methodist Church, since my credentials were in that denomination. This had all been decided through the Vermont Church Council without going through the regular Methodist channels. Rev. James Perry, our District Superintendent at that time, informed me that Methodist ministers have to be appointed by the Bishop instead of accepting a call from the church as in Congregational churches. After that gentle remonstrance to keep me straight on Methodist polity, he said, "But if you don't go, I don't know who will."

That is how I found myself moving my earthly goods to this village of 300 souls, six miles off the main highway thirty miles north of Burlington. Driving from Burlington to Waterville on an icy February morning over twisting gravel roads between rocky cliffs covered with sparkling icicles made me feel I was going into a very isolated place. The snow was so deep in that winter of 1942, I didn't know the town had sidewalks until spring finally arrived in late April.

Soon after moving to Waterville, I arranged an hour of Bible study each week in seven one and two-room elementary schools in the surrounding towns of Eden and Cambridge as well as in Waterville. In those years many schools provided for released time for a Protestant minister and a Catholic priest to teach religion. In the four one-room schools in the town of Eden, my Bible hour was done during school time, and there was no priest to teach the Catholic children. But the Catholic families welcomed the chance for their children to receive Bible teaching, as they found it difficult to attend church in nearby towns during the severe winters. That was before the Supreme Court had handed down a ruling making it illegal.

I was granted a license to preach, and I started the correspondence course provided for pastors without a B.D. degree. I managed to set up dental clinics for needy children as we had done in the Summer Projects. This pleased Mr. Turrell, as he felt the physical needs of children were just as important as their spiritual needs. I provided for several children to attend summer camps sponsored by the Methodist Church. At first I thought of my weekday classes as my main work and the Sunday church services as a supplementary part of my work. But I soon found that preparing sermons was helping to deepen my own faith. As I struggled to have sermons which would meet the needs of people facing the anxieties of war, I discovered the real message of the Bible. As we saw Hitler running rampant through Europe, I began to understand the doctrine of original sin. I saw the depths to which human beings can sink even in an era of widespread education in so-called civilized countries. Though I had shrunk from the crude imagery of the "revivalist" preaching I had heard in earlier years, I saw that within the metaphors was a profound truth in the doctrine of atonement which speaks to suffering people. When I had to preach the funeral of the younger brother of one of our members, killed in action, I understood anew the importance of the New Testament emphasis on the resurrection.

During the four and a half years I served there, I came to love the people of Waterville and they warmly welcomed me into their homes and their hearts. Fortunately I found living with the Davis family very enjoyable, and I had much in common with Emma in spite of our different backgrounds. She became a lifelong friend.

But when in 1946, I was asked to become the associate pastor of the Lake Region Parish in northeastern Vermont, I felt this was a call I couldn't refuse. It was a critical time in this new experiment of uniting the churches. Two denominations in

Barton had formed a United Church which would work cooperatively with the churches in 3 small towns in the area. They had begun this Larger Parish the year before, with a Congregational minister as the senior pastor and a young Methodist minister as the associate. This younger man found it difficult to work interdenominationally. So he asked to leave at the end of his first year. The district superintendent insisted he stay on another year as he felt he hadn't given it a fair trial. But somehow that Methodist pastor managed to get an appointment in Illinois and announced his resignation just after the Annual Conference. The Congregational minister decided it would be better to divide the two positions according to function rather than having two pastors trying to do the same kind of work. He looked for an associate who could concentrate on Christian education in the parish.

Two young Congregational women ministers in northern Vermont who had graduated from Hartford Seminary suggested he contact me since I was a Methodist who had a Masters' degree in Christian education. The District Superintendent had not been able to find a pastor since it was after the regular time of appointments. As I was not yet a full member of the conference, probably he hadn't considered me a possibility. So once again I was interviewed for this position before going through the regular channels. But as at Waterville, the Superintendent had to admit that if I didn't go, he didn't know who would. So he agreed to make the appointment.

Although it was difficult to leave the people in Waterville, I loved the challenge of leading the newly formed parish youth group and helping stimulate the teachers of the four church schools in the Lake Region Parish. During the summer months, we organized a parish-wide Vacation Bible School which drew about 100 children. There was a lake in each of the four towns. So our youth group had Sunday afternoon outings and worship services at one of the lakes or on a mountaintop in summer. At times I marveled that I was getting paid to enjoy all the scenic places where my work took me. I preached only about once a month except during the summer months when I preached every Sunday during the senior pastor's vacation. The four lakes in the area drew a large summer population which included many seminary professors and ministers from New York and other cities. Preparing sermons for those congregations kept me on my toes intellectually and spiritually.

When the war finally ended, I often heard thrilling accounts of Christians who volunteered to go to Germany to do relief work and to assist in healing the wounds of war. I wondered if I might be able to do something like that. I knew I would have to learn German and that seemed impossible for me. Then in 1948 my youngest brother and his wife were recruited by the Quakers to go to Tokyo for two years to do relief work, set up international forums, and teach English. His glowing letters about the Japanese people and the beautiful pictures of Japanese gardens fascinated me. He told me it wasn't necessary to learn the language for short term work as all the Japanese were eager to learn English. Having lived through the hatred that separated us during the war years, the possibility of building bridges of friendship with the Japanese people strongly appealed to me.

Although I had fully enjoyed my six and a half years in the Lake Region Parish, I decided to apply for a short term under our Methodist Mission Board which had initiated a program known as J-3's. Young people were to be sent to teach English in their church-related schools in Japan for three years. The age limit was 35 and I was almost 38. I knew that if I wanted to explore overseas work, I should not wait any longer. After I sent in my inquiry I was surprised to get an immediate response from the personnel secretary who said they welcomed more mature persons for the program. I found later that the arrival of a large number of "gung-ho" young college graduates who were eager to change the world had brought about conflict with some of the older pre-war missionaries who had returned after the war. Almost before I knew it, I was packing to go to Japan for three years to teach English and work with young people in the churches. After the difficult farewells to people in the Lake Region Parish where I had so thoroughly enjoyed the demanding but stimulating and fulfilling work, I spent six weeks of orientation on the familiar site of Hartford Seminary. Our leaders, Charles and Julie Germany, proved to be excellent role models as they had already spent one term in a rural area of Japan. In addition, we had ministers, linguists, and professors to give us courses to prepare us for living in another culture. The group of 48 young people were called A-3's, as we were to go to various Asian countries for three years to teach English and work with young people. Being with a group of recent college graduates was like a shot in the arm for me, as they were full of enthusiasm and ideals. They still believed that all things were possible.

Even though we were not required to learn the language for a three year term, we had a course in linguistics, and a three weeks tutoring session with a native speaker from our particular country. I was surprised to discover there were some full time missionaries who never mastered the language and had to depend on interpreters. The most important thing I learned was that as an adult learning a foreign language, you have to be willing to make a fool of yourself. I resolved to make my first priority learning as much of the Japanese language as I could. After making all those new friends and being filled with information and inspiration, I started my new career by taking a train from Xenia, Ohio, to New Orleans where we waited for a freighter to sail. There was a longshoreman's strike on the west coast which prevented us from embarking at Los Angeles as we had expected. I was happy to find that most of the twelve passengers on our freighter had been members of the Hartford orientation group. So the long journey by way of the Panama Canal with frequent stops to take on cargo, turned out to be a lot of fun as well as a continuation of our studies. Our daily routine included morning devotions, calisthenics on the upper deck, and a session of listening to tapes of our Japanese language textbook and repeating the sentence patterns. We took time for recreation and special celebrations like the time when we crossed the international date line.

After almost a month, we reached the port of Yokohama where we were met by Alice Cheney, a veteran missionary who helped us feel secure as we went through customs and were whisked to a mission house. It was a frightening experience to be in a taxi speeding recklessly through traffic on the wrong side of the road.

For the first time in my life, I understood how it feels to be illiterate. I could not read any signs, or newspapers. I couldn't understand anything people said. My resolve to learn the language was stronger than ever, as I began my new life in a totally strange situation.

3. First Impressions

The streets of Tokyo were teeming with people--women in drab kimonos, young women carrying babies on their backs, hordes of weary uniformed children on school trips sitting on their luggage as they waited in the train station. Streets were clogged with pedestrians and bicycles, as few roads had any sidewalks. Although I saw no ruins in the city, there were still a lot of unpaved roads in residential sections. I feared my shoes would not last too long walking on graveled roads. Removing our shoes on entering a house seemed a sensible custom. I woke up the second morning hearing the unfamiliar sound of the clop-clop of wooden clogs that were still worn by many people in those days. There was the noisy opening of sliding doors on neighboring houses. In this crowded city, the houses were wedged so closely together that we could hear doors opening and closing all along the street. People were leaving for work, and housewives were going out to do their morning chore of sweeping the street in front of their homes. Since it was approaching election day, we were wakened at the unearthly hour of 6:00 A. M. by the raucous sound of a politician's pitch, as he cruised the neighborhood to catch people before they left for work. He stood in the back of a pick-up truck, dressed in formal clothes with white gloves. Although I couldn't understand what he was saying, I was told he merely shouted his name and the post he was running for. Then he would bow to everyone in sight. I thought if I were a voter, I would decide not to vote for anyone who woke me at that hour.

I remember how strange everything seemed but also how comforting it was to have the missionaries receive us so graciously. They provided our meals and a good bed for the few days we spent in Tokyo. I wrote home that I found I knew more people in Tokyo than in New York. Since my younger brother, Neil and his wife, had lived there from 1948 to 1952, they had given me the addresses of some of their Quaker friends. I also looked up Ruth White, a classmate from college days who was working at the Ernie Pyle library, run by the American Occupation forces. I was able to attend the Saturday night folk dance at the Quaker Center where some of the young men whom Neil had taught were doing a great job of calling the square dances. I tried to telescope my first impressions in a letter to my family:

> "Beautiful tree-clad mountains which remind me of Vermont, neat vegetable patches and rice fields on every square inch of available land, lovely gardens with picturesque stone lanterns, curving pine trees trimmed so carefully that their needles grow in small clipped bunches; colorful dahlias, chrysanthemums and cosmos in abundance; people bowing low when they meet friends on the street, adorable chubby children who shout 'haroo' (hello) to every foreigner; mothers and grandmothers with babies on their backs; hundreds of school children on excursions, packing the trains and street cars; the strange sight of women working on roads and construction jobs; men hauling dirt in baskets hung from a bamboo pole slung across their shoulders. Everywhere too many people and not enough space; narrow roads meant for walking being stretched to let two big city buses meet each other. Everywhere there is such a mixture of old and new--women dressed in colorful kimonos wearing wooden clogs, and young girls in bright red sweaters, fashionable suits, and the latest style in shoes and hand-bags; older men wearing dark kimonos and others who look like New York business men. The stores present the same contrast--modern department stores stocked with electrical gadgets, lovely yard goods, and Max Factor make-up, but also little open-faced shops displaying everything from fresh fish to tea kettles."

The missionaries arranged for my ticket to Hiroshima where I had been assigned to teach, and they packed a lunch before we set off. Fortunately I didn't have to travel alone. There were two young short-term missionaries assigned to Korea who would be stationed temporarily in Hiroshima until the Korean war was over. Two veteran Korean missionaries, Miss Bessie Oliver and Miss Kate Cooper, were living in a rented Japanese house after being evacuated from Korea. Since there were a lot of Koreans in Hiroshima, they were assisting in the Korean church there. The new missionaries would be able to study the language with Korean tutors and help out at the church.

My first ride on a Japanese train was a new adventure, as we were surrounded by Japanese speaking people and all the announcements were in Japanese. It took all night and half of the next day although the same trip now takes only about a half day on the bullet train. I remember once when all the passengers seemed to be excited about something they saw out the window. Everyone was looking out on one side. When we followed their gaze, we saw the majestic Mt. Fuji in full splendor with its graceful lines rising from the horizon. I thought it was strange that the Japanese passengers should be so excited, as they must be used to seeing it. But I discovered later that on most days the mountain is shrouded in clouds. So the chance to see it in its pristine glory is indeed rare.

We were met at the train by Mary Bedell, Myra Anderson, and Joy Bourlay. Mary was what we sometimes called a "retread" from China, since all the missionaries had to leave when the Communists took over. Miss Anderson, whom we called Andy, was a soft spoken Southern woman who had served in Hiroshima before the war and was overjoyed to be back again. I was happy to know I would be living with Joy, a young Florida home economics teacher who had been in the same orientation group with me at Hartford. We found this was the second time they had come to the station to meet us. Somehow the Tokyo missionary had put us on a different train from the one they expected us to be on. Since meeting people and sending them off is very important among Japanese people, the school had sent a delegation of teachers and students along with the President, Miss Hamako Hirose, to welcome us. They were quite disappointed when we were not on that train, and they had to give up and go home.

The mission house where I was to live with three other women had been newly built on the downtown campus where the Hiroshima Girls' School had been founded in 1886. It had a big living room, dining room, modern kitchen, laundry room, downstairs lavatory, and a small "tatami" room with an adjoining Japanese style toilet, for our live-in maid. Upstairs there were four bedrooms all on the south side to take advantage of the sun. On the north side, there was a store room, a trunk room and a Western style bathroom plus a large linen closet. Each room had a nice closet with sliding doors. The windows were very wide, letting in lots of sunshine. The house was a sort of stucco on the outside with a tile roof. There was an American refrigerator, and a modern sink in the kitchen, but only a kerosene stove. However, we soon had a gas range installed. The house was located just beside the senior high school and the yard was still unfinished. Later we had a very nice small yard with flower beds and a fig tree beside our open porch. Having the living room and bedrooms on the south side made them much easier to heat. When the sun was out, even in early December, it might be warm enough for the students to enjoy eating their lunch outdoors.

Parallel to our house was a wooden dormitory which housed a small number of students whose homes were in country villages or on nearby islands. Most of the students commuted by train, bus, or bicycle. Every morning city buses from all directions spilled out long lines of uniformed students carrying their leather school bags, at the bus stop. It was named for our school, Hiroshima Jo Gakuin (Girls' School). From the main railroad station about half a mile down the street, other groups of students streamed into our school gates. They wore navy blue jumpers with plain white blouses and short box jackets. They were required to wear white ankle socks and black shoes. There were strict dress codes to make sure no one had lace or frills on their blouses, or fancy trimming on their socks. This was to make everyone feel equal. No permanents were allowed and no make-up. I remember one girl whose mother had to write a note assuring the teachers that her child was born with curly hair.

She was probably one of the few Japanese who look as if their ancestors came from the South Sea Islands.

When I was guided through the long hallway of the senior high building, they showed me the large teachers' room with many rows of desks crammed together, side by side. Every desk was piled high with papers, books, tea cups, and whatever items would be needed during the day. I wondered how anyone managed to concentrate on studying in this organized clutter. One of the things I soon discovered was that in Japanese society, group consciousness is very strong. There is much less individualism and sense of privacy than in America. They feel more comfortable doing things in groups. Their limited space makes it almost impossible to provide for individual rooms for teachers' study rooms. Another feature I noticed was the constant flow of green tea. A young office girl brought around a steaming kettle of tea to fill the handle-less cups on each desk. This happened not only the first thing in the morning, but also between classes, when all of us touched base during the break.

On my first morning, after I was introduced, we all stood up for a brief Bible reading, the singing of a hymn and a prayer, led by one of the Christian teachers. Then we all walked across the campus to the chapel for morning worship. There was a low hum of talking among the students during the prelude, but they sang the hymns beautifully. I recognized many of the tunes, but the words were in Japanese. As soon as I could read the phonetic alphabet, I would be able to sing with them even when I didn't know the meaning of all the words. I was determined to master those strange looking scratches as soon as possible. As I stood at the back of the chapel overlooking all those black-haired girls in their navy blue uniforms, I wondered if I would ever be able to communicate with them, and to have any idea of what they were thinking. I was more determined than ever to try to learn the language.

In some ways I felt quite at home living with three American women. But everything outside our house was strange. I found it difficult at first to be stared at by Japanese people wherever I went. Non-Japanese people were still a rarity outside the large urban areas. Sometimes mothers would point out to a small child, "Look, there's a gaijin." That word means literally *outside person*. I was most cordially received within our school. The staff were eager to have native speakers of English to help teach the students conversational English. Miss Hirose, the president, and both the principals could speak English very well. Among the English teachers were two Nisei (Japanese Americans) women whose English was very natural, as well as a few others who could communicate easily. Most of the other teachers, however, could not really speak English. They tried to use what few words they knew in helping me to feel welcome. I had pictured the students as being able to communicate in English, since I knew they had studied with American missionary teachers from their first year in junior high. But I soon found out how difficult it was for them to communicate in English.

I found constant reminders of the atom bomb. Most of the girls who wrote their life stories in my classes, mentioned someone in their family who had been killed at that time. Frequently I saw a young girl who was crippled or blind; a man with one leg, a woman with an unsightly burn on her face. I was told that the Japanese people had been relieved to find that the occupying army was there to help them rebuild their country and to become a truly democratic society. So they welcomed a chance to make a peaceful world and they were eager to learn all they could about democracy. The young people especially were determined to learn English as a way of communicating with the outside world. When they wrote speeches for the English speaking contests, their topic was nearly always world peace. They expressed their longing to make a world without war. This gave me hope that I could help to build bridges of friendship between our countries.

4. Learning the Japanese Language

Whenever people ask me, "How long did it take you to pick up Japanese?" my answer is, "I didn't pick it up, I dug it out." From the beginning of my career as a missionary, I found learning the language high on my priority list; yet it proved to be my most difficult. When people spoke admiringly of my skill in using chopsticks, I sometimes remarked, "If only learning to speak Japanese could be as easy as learning to handle chopsticks!"

During our six weeks orientation program at Hartford Seminary, Earl Stevick, who taught us basic linguistics, emphasized the importance of learning the language of the people where we lived. His aim was to help us to know how to go about learning a language. Although I had studied French in college, no one had helped me to be conscious of the different intonations in foreign languages. I think when I spoke French, I used English intonation as much as possible. He reminded us that we had learned our own language without textbooks and without rules of grammar, but we had a loving father and mother who repeated the words over and over for us. As an adult we would have to do that drilling ourselves if we were to remember new words and sentence structure.

During the last three weeks when we began learning simple greetings in Japanese with a young Japanese woman who was studying in America, I realized this was quite different from learning any of the Romance languages which are related to Latin and to English. The only word which sounded familiar was "ohaiyo" (sounds like Ohio) which means "good morning." Although children can use that one word as a greeting, adults are expected to add a polite ending, "gozaimasu," which is just the verb "to be." One of the difficulties in the language is learning the various endings and prefixes that make it sound polite.

The structure of sentences was entirely opposite from English, with the verb always coming at the end of the sentence instead of in the middle or at the beginning. Our textbook was one that had been used by the American GI's during the Occupation years. So we learned how to ask for beer and cigarettes, but we also learned some practical questions such as "Where is the station?" or "Where is the toilet?" One day we asked to have a Japanese-speaking table at dinner. But to our disappointment, almost all we knew how to say was "Please pass the salt." Nevertheless, by the time we left Hartford, we were full of hope and determination to persist in learning the language as much as possible.

Our long freighter voyage gave us time to practice Japanese every morning. We tried to "listen and repeat" as we were instructed on the tapes. What a letdown it was when we came close enough to tune in the Japanese news broadcasts from Tokyo. When I heard that rapid flow of Japanese, I could not recognize even one word that sounded familiar. I discovered later that news is always hard to understand, as they use a lot of short forms and specialized vocabulary.

As soon as we arrived in Yokohama, the battle with language began. Fortunately the older missionaries who met us at the dock, helped us to get through customs and to engage a taxi to the mission house where we were to stay a few days. Our hostesses were two young J-3s who were almost at the end of their short term. They seemed to know enough Japanese to instruct the maid, and to get around the city. I remember how helpless we felt when Esther, my roommate on the ship, and I were there alone. When the phone rang, she answered it. When the person greeted her with a flow of Japanese words, she used one of the words we had learned, "Wakarimasen" which means "I do not understand." But that must have made the caller think she did know some of the language. So she continued bombarding her with Japanese sentences. I heard Esther repeat "wakarimasen" about five times before the other person gave up. When I went to look up my former Ohio classmate who was working in the Ernie Pyle Library, I approached an intelligent looking Japanese man and asked in my best Japanese, "Ernie Pyle Library wa, doko ni arimasuka?" That meant, "Where is the Ernie Pyle Library?" Our teacher had told us when we didn't know the Japanese word, we could just insert English into a Japanese framework. But what I forgot was that you have to Japanize the pronunciation of English words. The man looked puzzled, but when he took out a notebook and asked me to write it down, his eyes lit up and he said, "Ah Aani Pairu Raibueri." Then he proceeded to tell me the directions in English. I'm sure I would not have been able to understand the directions in Japanese.

When I arrived in Hiroshima, I was again warmly welcomed by friendly missionaries and Japanese teachers who spoke English very well. But as soon as I entered the school to begin my classes, I ran into the language barrier. I had often heard that term, but for the first time I knew what it meant to feel as if there was a real wall which kept me from knowing what was occurring around me. Everything was done in Japanese. Information on the bulletin boards was in Japanese, and oral announcements were made in this unknown language. I couldn't use a phone book, or read a newspaper, or read signs at the bus stop. Mary Bedell, our China missionary, couldn't speak Japanese, but she could look at the signs and know what they meant in English. Japanese scholars adopted Chinese characters to form their written language even though they had to add grammatical endings to make it fit. They had created a phonetic alphabet by simplifying the characters. That meant learning this phonetic alphabet in addition to the many Chinese characters.

Another colleague, Mary McMillan, who taught in the college, was only one year older than I. But she had studied Japanese in the few years she had lived there before being sent home when World War II was imminent. During the war she had worked with Japanese-American people in the "relocation camps" in the American west. When I heard her chatting away in Japanese to the people around her, I wondered if I would ever reach that level of fluency.

Although the mission board did not send us to language school, as short-termers, they urged us to have a Japanese tutor at their expense. I was lucky to be able to study about five hours a week with two tutors. My term overlapped with Dorothy Seest, the young woman whose place I would be taking. So my teaching hours were few at first. I was pleased when Mr. Niwa, who was reputed to be the best teacher of Japanese as a foreign language in the city, agreed to take me on. But I was told I should study with a woman also, as men's language was somewhat different from polite women's language. They used softer words, but with my untrained ear, I couldn't tell what words were softer.

When Andy took me to meet Pastor Harano whose name I had received from a Canadian pastor whom I knew in Vermont, I was delighted to have him recommend his wife as a tutor. She had graduated from our school in the pre-war years and she had taken the training for a kindergarten teacher at the junior college which became Seiwa Women's College in Kobe. She was shy about using English but she understood my English very well.

At first the simplest errand took about twice the time expected. When I went to the post office to buy stamps, I had to write down just what I wanted to order. Sometimes I was provoked when the postal clerk answered me in English. He didn't seem to realize I was trying hard to learn how to use the language. Since our cook could not speak any English, I had to use my Japanese when it was my turn to plan menus. I found myself using my hands a lot, and often I ended up demonstrating the recipe by doing it myself.

About twice a month I attended the after-school teachers' meeting which seemed to go on forever. The whole faculty had to discuss everything -- from schedules to school policy to individual discipline problems. They didn't vote on decisions but they went round and round until they came to a consensus. At first I tried to get a missionary or an English-speaking Japanese to interpret for me. But if they spoke it in an undertone, that was a disruption of the meeting, and if someone wrote the gist of the meeting on a note pad, that meant she could not take part in the discussion. When I realized this was an imposition on them, I just sat there and listened. I contented myself with looking up words in my small dictionary. But often there was a half page or more of words with the same sound. And of course by the time I found the word, they had gone on to another topic.

One thing I looked forward to was the tea and cakes which the office girl brought around.   But even when they put the refreshments in front of each teacher, it seemed that it wasn't polite to partake of them right away. I tried to wait until others took up their teacups and started eating the cake. Usually the head teacher who was a man, was the one to begin. I wanted to wait for the first woman, but some of them never did eat the cake. Instead, they wrapped it up and took it home. At that time the cakes were beautiful creations of bean paste and sugar, but the taste was rather "blah." However I welcomed anything to break the boredom of that long ordeal. I persisted in going to the meetings, as I wanted the teachers to know I really hoped to be a part of the life of the school.

Attending church worship services every Sunday was another ordeal. Teaching my English Bible class to college students was enjoyable and challenging, but sitting through the long sermon afterwards was very difficult. I discovered I had chosen the church where the sermons were especially long. They always lasted 40 to 50 minutes. And even when the benediction came, the end was not yet, as the pastor made innumerable announcements. Once I looked up a word which I heard him say many times, thinking it might give me a clue to his topic. To my dismay I found the word meant "but" or "however." I could read the day's Scripture in my English Bible, and I worked hard at memorizing the Lord's Prayer in Japanese. But eventually I contented myself by doing my own meditation and prayer while the minister was preaching.

Several of the church members could speak English and they were always helpful and friendly during the time of fellowship after the service. I was able to sing the hymns as soon as I had learned the phonetic alphabet, as these symbols (kana) were printed above the Chinese characters. So I could sing even if I didn't know the meaning.   Quite often the hymns were translations from English or German. So I knew the meaning and when I directed the choir, I tried to help the young people to sing them with expression. Most of them understood English so that we could get along well. Of course this meant that it was very late by the time I got home for dinner. No one else seemed to worry about eating. Probably some of the young people ducked out of church between the various events to eat a bowl of noodles at one of the many shops in the area.

Since I was pushing 40 by the time I went to Japan, I decided to concentrate on speaking the language instead of trying to master both the speaking and the writing and reading. I did learn the phonetic alphabet mainly by seeing it every day in the hymnal which we used in chapel. They had created this phonetic alphabet (kana) by simplifying some of the Chinese characters, though they were not simple for me. The Chinese characters (kanji) were really pictures which conveyed a meaning. But the phonetic "kana" indicated a sound which was always the same.

Japanese has only 5 vowel sounds plus "n" which becomes a vowel when it occurs at the end of words. To make this alphabet, they put each consonant in front of those 5 vowels. So we learned "ka, ki, ke, ko, ku" and on through the various consonants. All these simplified Chinese characters looked so much alike to me that it took awhile to learn them. Our young tutor in Hartford had told us blithely that we could sit down and learn them in one evening. But it certainly took me much longer. One helpful method was using children's blocks which had the "kana" on one side and the English alphabet on the other side. To make it more complex, there was a second phonetic alphabet "katakana" used just for foreign words and names. These were only slightly different from the regular phonetic alphabet known as "hiragana".

The Japanese have adopted many English words, but they put them into their sound system. In some countries they have made up new words when new technology such as radio and TV were introduced, but in Japan they use "rajio" and "terebi" etc. Knife, fork and spoon are called by their English names. When it comes to baseball which was introduced by Americans early in the 20th century, everything is in Japanized English. Strike one becomes "sutoraiku wan" and foul ball becomes "fauro boru." They often take English or German words and give them a special meaning. The word mansion becomes a condominium in a high rise building. They use the German word for work, "arbeit" to mean part time work for students, or work without fringe benefits. When that word is shortened from "arubaito" it becomes "baito" and the English word strike "sutoraiku" becomes "suto" which is of course very puzzling to the foreigner.

Verbs seemed very complicated, as we had to learn six different endings to form various tenses and moods. Then we had to learn three or four sets of verbs with the same meaning but with different levels of politeness. There is an honorific form used when speaking to someone older or more important than oneself. There is a humble form when speaking about yourself or your family, and what is called a plain form used among intimates. This also applies to some nouns. A man should use the word "kanai" to speak about his own wife, but he calls another person's wife "okusan." Actually both words mean "inside person" which gives a clue as to how they viewed women in traditional society. My Japanese teacher tried to explain the nuance of the word "kanai" by saying it means "my silly goose of a wife." Of course he was half joking, but it did convey something like that. Sometimes a man uses the very rough sound of "ooi" when calling his wife. This always made Andy very indignant. One of the first things I learned was how to introduce myself. This was always a custom in a new group. I could say, "My name is Doris Hartman, and I am a teacher at Hiroshima Jo Gakuin."

But after I did this at a teachers' meeting, one of the older missionaries explained that I should have used the humble word for teacher instead of the word we used for others. All the teachers used the term "sensei" when speaking to each other. They tend to use titles more than personal names. But in speaking of myself, I should have used the plain word, "kiyoshi."

Once when my teacher was trying to explain about using different words for those above me and below me, I told him I wanted to be democratic. I didn't want to judge who was above me and who was below me. As a Christian, I believe that all people are equal in the sight of God. But my teacher who was also a Christian said it would sound silly to use very polite forms when speaking to the garbage man, for example. I found that to be true when I tried out a very polite phrase on my junior high students in an informal situation. They giggled because I had used language too polite when speaking to people younger than myself.

Another difficulty was in learning to count. Most of the American GI's thought they could count in Japanese. But I soon discovered there had to be a different ending on each number depending on whether you were counting thin things, flat things, animals, people, and birds and so on "ad infinitum." Then just for good measure, there is another whole set of numerals which sound like entirely different words.

Another difference is in the use of personal pronouns. The pronouns for "I," "you," "he," and "she" are rarely used. For example when I wanted to say "My shoulders hurt", I put in the word for my, but the teacher laughed, saying, "Of course they are your shoulders, as you wouldn't know if someone else's shoulders hurt."

There is a word for "You" (anata), but it is seldom used except between husband and wife. They often use third person nouns even when speaking directly to another person. For example, instead of saying, "Are you going?" it comes out "Is sensei (teacher) going?" Or when speaking to a married woman, they would use "okusan" instead of "you."

One complication in reading Japanese is that each character has a Chinese reading and a Japanese reading. For example, the Japanese word for east is "higashi," but the Chinese reading is "tou." When this is combined with another syllable to make a word, they use the Chinese reading. Tokyo means "eastern capital." So when you use "higashi" combined with the word "kyo" it becomes "tou." How often I wished those early Japanese scholars had just gone to some of the European countries to get their written language instead of to China! At least they would have had an alphabet similar to ours. Even Japanese people often do not know how to read a person's name. The first syllable of my friend, Miss Saikyo's name means "west." The Japanese word is "nishi", but since it is combined with another syllable it becomes the Chinese "sai."

Imagine how complicated it has been to keep records and files in offices. Until the time of computers, very few people could use a Japanese typewriter. It was a large bulky machine which was more like a printing press than a typewriter. They put in some of the characters as they needed them. The present day word processor seems like magic. They use the English alphabet for the keyboard. But the computer can change these to Chinese characters. When there are words that have the same sound but different meaning, the computer brings up all the possible characters at the flip of a button. The typist, of course, has to know which one is correct in that context.

People from other countries often suggest using only the phonetic alphabet and doing away with the Chinese characters known as "kanji." But the objection always is that there are too many words which sound the same. Seeing the "kanji" makes the meaning clear at once. Even on their TV newscasts they always have a printed commentary at the bottom of the screen when a person is speaking. I believe another reason for not giving up "kanji" is that educated people have a vested interest in keeping them. Imagine spending half your life mastering these thousands of characters only to have them wiped out.

The whole system of writing is an art as well as a way of communication. Children enter contests to see who can write the most artistically. Often the characters are used on scrolls instead of pictures, as an art form. One of our Japanese teachers said that looking at the characters is like looking through a window to receive knowledge. A foreign student replied that to him they were like prison walls which kept him out. That expressed my feelings in the early years.

By the end of my first three years, I could get around town. I could use the transportation, do the shopping, and understand answers when I asked directions. I could carry on simple conversations, but it was hard to express my inmost thoughts or to make a speech or understand formal lectures. But at least I had made a beginning on breaking down that awful language barrier.

5.   Early Days In Hiroshima

What would it be like in the city of Hiroshima just seven years after the first atom bomb had devastated the city? I was rather surprised to see that it seemed to have been totally rebuilt when I arrived at the temporary railroad station in October of 1952. The American Occupation had just ended. The only reminder of those days was the special waiting room where an English-speaking attendant was on duty. When I saw pictures of the city as it looked after the bombing, it seemed to be just a heap of rubble, with a few reinforced concrete shells of buildings left standing like skeletons.

But when I arrived, I was amazed to see the downtown full of modern buildings with almost no ruins except the dome that had been left as a memorial at the epicenter of where the bomb fell. Many of these were temporary buildings that were replaced with more sturdy reinforced concrete buildings after a few years. Our school was in the process of being rebuilt. The temporary barracks that housed the junior high were just being replaced by a brand new reinforced concrete junior high building. The senior high students were still in a temporary wooden building, but they had a new chapel next door on the campus. The junior high chapel, the earliest post war building to be constructed, was a wooden structure which served also as their gymnasium.

Naturally I felt some trepidation when I traveled around the city and mingled with people on the streetcars. From the beginning, I knew what it was like to be a foreigner. Since all Japanese have black hair and dark eyes, there is no way that an American person can hide her identity. It took me awhile to get used to having people stare at me, but I didn't experience hostility. To my surprise, most Japanese were eager to learn from Americans as they wanted to create a true democracy where they could live in peace. They were eager to learn English so they could communicate with the rest of the world.

Pastors of churches who were weary from trying to rebuild after the war were glad to have young missionaries who could teach an English Bible class. There was a boom in Christianity as they were disillusioned with state Shintoism which had led them into a futile war. Non-Christians were also eager to learn from Americans and I was asked to speak by various secular groups. Sometimes a teacher from a rural school asked the missionaries to speak to their students after school. They always asked many questions about America. Some women's groups asked me to teach them American cooking.

Even though the buildings had been replaced, the roads were still unfinished. I had to remember to wear rain boots not only on the day it rained, but also on the day after, as everything was a sea of mud. There were not many sidewalks, and people still used the roads for walking as they did in the days before automobiles. So the drivers laid on their horns as they tried to weave their way through the mass of pedestrians. There were no private cars except those owned by banks or schools or businesses. There were buses, trucks, taxis, and even a few horse and wagons.

I was rather scared to ride in the taxis, as they barreled along at reckless speed intent on getting as many fares as they could. One of their tricks for producing a smooth ride was to set their wheels exactly on the streetcar tracks and stay there until one of the trolleys came in sight. But even more frightening was their desire to use the strip of paved road still left on one side of the road. It was like a game of "chicken" to see how long they could stay on it when an oncoming taxi had the same idea. The cheapest sort of taxi was a three-wheeled vehicle which was a kind of glorified motorcycle attached to a back seat with a canvas curtain to keep out the rain. They were nicknamed "bata-bata" and people warned me about using them, as they could overturn very easily.

Riding in a bus at rush hour presented still other problems. There was always a young girl or boy recruited from junior high graduates who couldn't go on to high school who acted as conductors. They helped older people and children get on and off the buses which had very high steps unsuited to a population of short people. Then they made the rounds to sell tickets to the passengers, to call out the stations, and to stick their heads out the window to let the driver know if he would clear the overhanging eaves of houses flush with the narrow roads.

They literally stuffed people in at every stop. When I was sure not one more person could board the bus, the conductor cheerily shouted for everyone to squeeze back a little more. To my surprise, five or six people would find a toehold somewhere. The last ones might be perched on the steps by the front door. The bus girl would put one foot on the bottom step, and with her other foot hanging in the air, she would instruct the driver to let her roll. That was one of the many times when they used an English word. They called out "all light, all light" When I mentioned to my teacher that it sounded like English, he assured me they were saying all right. During rainy season, the smell of damp wool school uniforms made the ride something I endured until I could reach my destination.

In contrast, today's buses have a machine that spews out a ticket when the passenger drops in the coins, with a change maker machine instead of a kindly conductor. The taped voice of a young woman calls out the bus stops, and reminds everyone "Be sure not to leave any items on the bus when you get off."

The new mayor of the city, Mr. Hamai, had been a rather unimportant subordinate in city government. As one of the few survivors, he felt he had a real mission to rebuild the city. He developed a well-thought-out plan which would take 25 years to accomplish. He decided to merge two narrow roads to make one wide boulevard in the downtown section. At first there was one squatter's hut perched on a piece of land right in front of the main department store. All traffic had to go around it and road construction couldn't begin until they persuaded him to leave.

Before they began making a concrete road, they had to move every inch of streetcar track from one side to the middle of the wide road. Big machinery was non-existent at that time. So everything was done by hand. Putting in small squares of concrete seemed to proceed at a snail's pace. Instead of traffic lights, a policeman stood on a small box in the center of the main intersection downtown. The graceful movements of the officer as he blew his whistle and changed his stance to indicate the stopped traffic could move, and the other side should stop reminded me of a ballet dancer. He seemed to be lord of all he surveyed, as he proudly controlled the destinies of all the drivers.

Soon after I arrived, I purchased a brand new bicycle for the princely sum of about $30, using special gifts I had received from my home church. It was far easier to get around town by bicycle in those days than it is on today's wide streets which are filled with endless cars. At first I was a bit afraid, but I soon realized they were used to treating bicycles like any other vehicle. So when I boldly held out my hand to signal a turn, I knew the cars would wait. Since the main part of the city is quite flat, it was an ideal place for bicycling, once I got used to traveling on the left side. Dottie Seest, who had an old battered bike, referred to my new shiny one as my "Cadillac." I was always careful to lock it up in our little bicycle garage which they had built into the mission house under a stairway.

Somehow they managed to have bus routes to all the outlying towns extending into mountainous areas. I wrote in one of my letters that Japan had 20th century buses traveling on 15th century roads. Most people traveled long distances by train. Their trains connecting the main cities were efficient, but at that time there were not enough coaches. Experienced travelers would arrive at the platform very early. Then one of their party would dash into the coach to grab seats as soon as the door opened, while another one passed the luggage through the open window. Within a few minutes all the seats were taken, leaving the rest of the people to stand in the aisles, crammed into both ends of the coach like sardines. At times, it was actually hard to breathe. Fortunately I was taller than most of those around me, which enabled me to be in an upper layer of the atmosphere.

I had heard of the Japanese people's love of nature and their expertise at gardening. Now I saw many examples of this. They were just finishing our new junior high school building when I arrived. But even before the building was finished, they had planted what looked like full-grown trees in the narrow strip of yard at the front. That spring there was a plum tree in full bloom, though it had been put in the ground just a short time before. I also noticed that workmen were busy planting rows of trees along the wide road beside our school, even before any paving was done. Since most of the big trees in the city had been destroyed, it was quite important to have shade trees in place as soon as possible. But I couldn't help thinking that in America, we would probably think having a paved road came first, and after that, if there were enough funds, we could plant trees. In one of my early letters, I commented on their love of flowers:

"Wherever you go, you see evidence of the deep love of flowers. A small wall vase filled with fresh flowers decorates most city buses. Flower arrangements give beauty and color to post offices and other public buildings. At our railroad station they have built a sort of 'tokonoma' --the Japanese word for the alcove or beauty spot in each home--where beautiful flower arrangements are displayed continuously. At school, each classroom has a vase of flowers on the teacher's desk. For special occasions in the chapel, they use a huge blue pottery vase in which they arrange large branches and flowers. At our graduation ceremony last week, they used the delicate pink plum blossoms mixed with pink carnations and greenery."

Almost everyone was poor in those early post-war years. Although my salary was very low by American standards, I felt as if I was quite affluent compared to the Japanese teachers. At that time the exchange rate was pegged at 360 yen to the dollar, whereas in recent years it fluctuates between 80 and 150 yen per dollar. One young missionary told me her students commented that she wore a different dress everyday. After that, she tried to wear one outfit for about a week or so. The one luxury that tempted me was to use the cheap taxis to get around town. But I tried to use streetcars and buses in the same way most Japanese people did. After I acquired a bicycle, I could use that except on rainy days.

Many women had traded expensive kimonos for food in the difficult days just after the defeat. One teacher told me she remembered when department stores displayed only string in their show windows. But the Korean War had begun to help their economy, and department store windows had beautiful displays in them.

We had two maids in our mission house to do the work for the four women who lived there. That seemed like an unnecessary luxury. But our American supervisor assured us that it would take an interminable amount of time just to do the grocery shopping. Instead of a large supermarket, there was a fish shop, a meat shop, a green grocer, a fruit store, a bakery, etc. We were told we had been sent to Japan to teach school which would take all our time. Our older maid had been employed by the founder of our school and had served the missionaries faithfully for many years. After the war, her daughter who became a war widow needed employment, and she did the house cleaning and preparation of vegetables to assist her mother.

Even though Hiroshima had a population of about half a million at that time, the city did not have a complete sewage system. Only those who could afford a septic tank could have indoor plumbing. Because of limited space, houses were built with an old fashioned toilet attached to the house instead of in the back yard as they used to be in America. I couldn't help admiring the ingenious methods they used to counteract the unpleasant odors with various liquid and powdered chemicals. Another method was to install a pipe projecting through the roof of the small cubicle, with an electric fan at the top to help the odors escape. What I found most difficult in our school was the lack of any heat, except for a hibachi in the teacher's room where we all had a desk. A "hibachi" is a large round crock filled with white sand on which two or three sticks of smoldering charcoal are placed after they have been kindled in a small clay pot which has a draft in the bottom. Of course this bit of charcoal doesn't change the temperature of the room. But people can warm their hands over it. Everyone wore enough layers of wool to keep their body warm, but it felt good to place our cold hands over the hot coals. At some time during my first three years, they installed small wood-burning metal stoves in the classrooms. This was an improvement, but those who sat near the stove were much too hot, and those who sat far away felt little heat at all. By the time I started my second term at the school, they had put in steam heat in most of the buildings except for the chapel. That has changed now, because they celebrated the 100th anniversary in 1986 by constructing a brand new chapel which has steam heat. It also has a real pipe organ from Germany.

Another lack in most homes was hot water heaters. Because a Japanese bath is so important to them, they had devised a method for heating water for the bath before they had it for washing dishes. Under the metal tub installed in the bathroom, there was a small firebox which opened outside by the front door. The tub was filled with water in the early evening. Then they started a fire by using paper and kindling over which they placed artificial logs made of pressed sawdust. There was a cold water faucet over the tub to be used to cool the water if it was too hot. Most housewives washed dishes and clothes in cold water, though they had very good detergents to make suds. When I moved out to Furuichi, one of my neighbors was still doing her laundry in a tub using a washboard in the small space outside her kitchen door. In winter she always had chapped hands. Fortunately she persuaded her husband to buy an electric washer. During the 1960s, electric appliances were becoming more widely used, but they still used cold water.

Taking a bath in Japan is a ritual that has an important place in everyone's daily schedule. It is not just to maintain cleanliness. It is also a time to relax and to let the cares of the day fall away. Whenever there is a conference extending over a few days, there is time allotted to the bath each day as an important part of the schedule. It is important to know the correct routine. First one washes the complete body using lots of soap, while sitting on a low stool on the tile floor which is well drained. The next step is to rinse thoroughly by dipping a small basin into the tub and splashing it all over the body. (In recent years there are hand-held showers for rinsing). Then the person climbs into the tub for a long soak. There is a piece of wood or plastic on which to sit with knees touching the chin in hot water up to the neck. The whole family soaks in the same water during one evening. So it is important to rinse well as there shouldn't be any scum on the water. Young children usually take turns sharing the tub with the mother and/or the father. This is a time that is cherished by the children. I never heard of a child who hated to take a bath. Parents are always rather sad when the children become too self-conscious to share the bath with them.

Nowadays most people have hot water tanks fueled by gas or electricity as we do, and the tub is more likely to be plastic than the old fashioned metal tubs. In a hotel, there is often a fairly large bath where several people can share in soaking and relaxing. It resembles a small shallow swimming pool. Once I became used to the very high temperature of the Japanese "ofuro" (the word for bath), I looked forward to it as the only time I was really warm in the winter. If the water is just warm enough to be comfortable, it soon becomes lukewarm. But when I learned to plunge into the hot water as we do into a cold swimming pool, then it becomes just right after a short time. It really warms the blood stream. So the trick is to get into bed right away and stay warm all night.

6.   English Teacher In Japan

Fortunately I was initiated into my English classes gradually, as my term overlapped with the J-3 Dorothy Seest, whom I was to replace. I needed a lot of help, as I had very little training in teaching English as a foreign language. I soon discovered their problems were quite different from those of my English classes in Ohio. I could see that studying English for one period five days a week from junior high through high school didn't mean they could converse in it. They learned to read, to translate, and to figure out difficult grammatical problems which might appear on entrance exams. But only the ones I called the "eager beavers" learned to speak it.

The sheer numbers in my classes overwhelmed me--about 50 in each class. Our role as native speakers was to use the same text that had been introduced by the Japanese English teachers. We tried to find ways to drill them in using the sentence patterns they had learned. I often told them they had a lot of English in their heads, but my job was to help them get it into their mouths. I spent time helping them to place their tongues and their lips in the proper way to make sounds that were not in their own language. All this was new to me also, but there were many good books to help me in ways of doing it.

The students had their Japanese teacher five days a week, but there was only one period a week for oral drill by the foreign teachers. Dividing the first year junior high students into two divisions, using two foreign teachers, was a help. But even with 29 in the class, it was almost impossible to have everyone answer a question more than once or twice during the period. I often resorted to having them answer in chorus. But then I couldn't tell who really knew the answer. I found myself speaking more and more slowly to be sure they understood me. But our task was to help them get used to hearing English at natural speed. So I tried to guard against my tendency to slow down.

Since they had been in large classes ever since kindergarten, the students were used to a good deal of regimentation. They had been taught to stand when the teacher entered, and at a signal from the leader, everyone bowed and gave their greetings. The main discipline problem was how to keep the brightest students from telling the answers to the weaker students. I had to insist that only the person whose name I called was to give the answer.

Just copying all those Japanese names in my grade books and trying to memorize them was a major chore. Most of them had long names of many syllables, all entirely alien to me. I really worked late into the night when grading time came. Of course I wrote their names in the Romanized alphabet which they called "Romaji." In my English classes they wrote their names that way on their papers.

One great frustration was having my one class a week (for each group) wiped out when a holiday fell on that date. There were other interruptions such as school outings, culture day, and the big fall field day known as "undokai" which cut into class time. Sometimes these off days came as a surprise to me, since the Japanese teachers forgot that notices on bulletin boards and oral announcements meant nothing to me. Eventually we worked out a system whereby the principal gave us the schedule in English, ahead of time.

I did have a chance to teach conversational English to senior high girls in small classes of 10 or 12. The missionary teachers had worked out a special English course as an elective which could be chosen in place of home economics. These classes which we met three times a week were pure pleasure. There was time to do creative activities such as skits, book reports, oral speeches, and writing episodes from their life stories.

My classes concentrated on spoken English, but I often assigned book reports on simple children's books or short essays about their life stories. Sometimes they acted out folk tales. They loved dramatizing stories, and they had a real flair for making costumes. I can still see Cinderella in a lovely white gown when she dressed for the ball. To our disappointment, the Japanese teachers voted to discontinue this elective after a few years, as they feared those students would not have enough time to study for college entrance exams. When I retired almost 30 years later, a group of those special English students--then middle-aged women--entertained me at a lovely dinner. They still spoke good English and most of them were using it in their careers or as tutors to neighborhood children.

As soon as I arrived, I was besieged with requests to teach English--in church night schools, the YM and YW classes, as well as English Bible classes at churches and universities. This helped to work off my frustration with the many interruptions which decreased my hours in our school system. The churches were full of young people. Many of them were seeking for a new faith by which to live, as well as a chance to practice their English.

In one of my earliest letters, I reported on my various extra-curricular activities: an after-school Bible class for high school girls, serving as advisor to the small YWCA which was one of our school clubs, and advising the English Speaking Society (known as ESS). I remember being surprised that they always spoke Japanese even though they called it an English Speaking Society. But they did take part in oratorical contests in English at various schools around the city.

At the request of Andy, I agreed to teach English in the church night school where she was involved. I remember the first time I set out to get there by myself. She told me to look for the character on the front of the streetcar that looked like three little boxes. With that little bit of knowledge, along with the name of the correct car stop, I managed to arrive at the right place. I did feel a moment of panic, wondering what would happen if I had taken the wrong car, and had ended up in an unknown part of the city. With my limited Japanese, would I ever find my way back? It never happened, but if it had, I am sure someone would have guided me back to our school, which was well known in the city. Japanese people often went out of their way to guide a foreigner to the right place.

After a few weeks, I took on a Sunday morning English Bible class at the church which I attended, as well as directing a choir of young people twice a month after the service. Every Sunday night I went over to the nearby dormitory to lead the girls in singing English hymns, at the request of the pleasant young woman teacher who was in charge. A British missionary asked me to take over her large English Bible class at Hiroshima University while she was on furlough. There were 20 or more students who came faithfully each week, and they had many questions. Probably for many of them, it was a fleeting experience, but I do know several students who came into the church through the influence of that class.

In addition to these teaching jobs, I was studying Japanese with two different tutors about five times a week. I was also taking lessons on the new Hammond organ in the chapel. Our music missionary, Grace Wilson, had persuaded the Methodist women from her home state of Iowa to donate this organ for the newly built chapel. It was the only organ in the city except for the pipe organ at the nearby Catholic music college. Since Grace would be leaving for her furlough in a few months, she hoped to teach me to play the hymns for chapel. At that time, there were no students who could play the organ, although many were studying piano. One of the hardest things I ever did was to coordinate my hands and feet on that organ. As the days got colder, it took sheer determination to practice in that unheated auditorium. Even the small electric heater I placed near my feet hardly made any difference.

One of the pleasant activities I enjoyed was singing in the massed chorus to prepare for the community "Messiah" which Grace had initiated. They were singing it in Japanese, but she wrote out the syllables in the Romanized alphabet to enable me to follow along. We could see our breath as we practiced in that chilly auditorium, but no one complained. I couldn't help recalling how the mothers of our Sunday School children in Vermont had objected to having us practice for the Christmas program when the temperature was about 65 degrees in our church. When we finally presented our Christmas oratorio to an enthusiastic audience in early December, our efforts seemed worthwhile.

Schools begin in April and end in March. I never was sure why this time schedule was chosen. One explanation, which fits in with the Japanese reverence for nature, is that it seems appropriate for young children to begin their studies when new life is springing up in the world of nature around them. I felt it would have been better to use the months of March and April while the days were conducive to study instead of having to drag through the steamy hot days of the June and July rainy season. The month of February is broken up because of seniors taking college entrance exams.

Their August vacation could not be carefree as all students were given summer homework. Parents had to see that the children spent a few hours each morning filling in their special workbooks. Teachers and students both had to report back to school for one or two days in August to have their work checked. College students faced term examinations soon after returning in September. That seemed to ruin their August vacation because even if they didn't study, they had a guilty feeling they should be studying.

I came to dislike the whole system of exams intensely, as it tends to dominate the way subjects are taught all the way through school. It puts so much pressure on the seniors that their whole year is given over to intensive memorizing and rote learning instead of having fun, making friends, or trying out their creative ideas. The week given over to entrance exams at each college is known as "hell week," as those exams are crafted to keep students from getting in. Actually there are enough colleges for everyone, but almost everyone wants to get into the top few. These are the big name schools in Tokyo and Kyoto that provide an open door to jobs in the biggest companies, which have the best fringe benefits and chance for promotion. This is not quite so true for young women, as they often expect to have a job for just a few years until they get married. That is beginning to change, however, as more women are determined to have both marriage and a career.

The reckoning day comes some time in March. In front of any university one can see extended bulletin boards filled with numbers, indicating those who passed. Crowds of young people and their parents eagerly scan them to see if their assigned number is there. Soon some of them are jumping up and down and hugging each other. But those whose numbers are not on the board, will dissolve in tears and hurry away. There are always some that commit suicide or suffer deep depression if they fail. But many of them steel themselves to try again the following year. They become "ronin" --a term used in feudal times for a warrior without a master. So that means going to a cram school where they learn how to be a good test taker. It seems such a waste to have so many young people cramming facts and figures instead of allowing them to enter college and letting them sink or swim.

High school graduation comes on the first of March, though the underclass students continue until about the middle of the month. Attending my first graduation was quite an occasion. At the urging of one of the young missionaries, I borrowed a kimono and had the dormitory matron dress me up. I found that it is a very complicated process beginning with the under kimono. Then it requires lots of strings to hold everything together, ending with the elaborate folding and tucking required to hold the gorgeous "obi" (sash) in place. There are also special socks called "tabi" which fit into the footwear known as "zori." The students got a kick out of seeing these foreigners in kimono, and they were eager to take our pictures. Ironically the other teachers all wore dark suits, though many of the mothers came in kimono. Many women still could not afford to buy a kimono which cost around $50 at that time. At present they are more likely to be around $1000 and up.

I soon discovered there are formal ceremonies to mark the beginning and the end of every endeavor. There is a set ceremony at the beginning of each semester as well as a closing ceremony for those who continue after commencement. Naturally, the most solemn one is the graduation, when all the parents attend if possible. Miss Hirose wore her robe with its colorful doctoral hood which she had earned at Columbia University. The students all wore their navy blue uniforms with spotless white blouses.

In addition to the speeches by the president, the chairman of the board, the PTA president, and the principal, one girl from the junior class gave a farewell to the seniors, and one senior responded. A formal speech for such an occasion is written in beautiful calligraphy on a long scroll which is folded up and fitted into a cover. When the girl ascended to the stage, she very slowly and deliberately took it out of the cover, and unfolded it. Then she read it from top to bottom. When she finished, she carefully folded it again and put it into the folder and presented it to the president. Taking a few steps back, she bowed to the president and the other notables on the stage, then to the audience, before making her way down the steps. She must have felt very nervous, as all this was done in a solemn silence with all eyes fixed on her. For me it was a real test of endurance to sit through that long ceremony--in a tight kimono--without understanding much at all. But the newness of the whole occasion kept me from being bored. When the seniors marched out of the auditorium, many were weeping. Their whole lives centered around their school, and leaving it evoked great sadness. As we all milled about on the school grounds afterwards, I was pleasantly surprised when many of the mothers came to me and bowed low, saying, "Thank you for teaching my daughter." I could understand that much in Japanese. I couldn't help thinking that teaching school in America was never like this.

7.   Unfamiliar Sights and Sounds

Bicyclists peddling their wares in a loud voice day and night or by playing music struck me as very strange. Every morning the tofu peddler bicycled around the neighborhood carrying six-inch squares of tofu in a tub of water on his sidecar. His cheery long-drawn-out cry, "Toofu-Toofu" alerted the housewives to bring their pans and bowls in which to put the amount needed for their morning soup. This was prepared by combining fish stock and a brown paste of fermented beans (miso) with vegetables and cubes of tofu to make a nourishing breakfast. Other staples on the menu were rice and pickles and perhaps black crisp seaweed strips dipped in soy sauce. One favorite kind of pickles is made from the large white radishes (daikon) soaked in brine over a long period of time. Breakfast in Japan is not so different from any other meal, so it often includes fish and vegetables.

The puffed rice man literally puffed the rice a housewife brought to him by heating it over bellows in his sidecar which caused the rice to explode like popcorn. Then it was propelled into a rigid wire container above the heatcr. Unlike popping corn, the kernels all exploded at once, making a product just like our puffed rice. Children loved to stand around--with hands over their ears--to wait for the loud explosion. We liked it for morning cereal, but the children preferred the tasty confection he made by dipping it into a sugar and water syrup which he stirred up over his fire.

The sweet potato woman often came by our high school, pulling her handcart with a wood fire container over which she roasted sweet potatoes in a large pot. It was considered a welcome snack on a winter afternoon when we were grading papers in the teachers' room after school. Whoever was sent out to buy them would return with the potatoes wrapped in newspapers, hot and aromatic. We peeled them with our fingers sand ate them without any trimmings. There were some Japanese people who said they had lived on sweet potatoes during the war years when rice was rationed and they never wanted to see one again.

Not only food was peddled by bicycle, but also entertainment. One person, who could gather a crowd of youngsters whenever he appeared, was the "kami shibai" man--literally, paper theater. He carried a stack of fairly good-sized cardboard pictures depicting favorite folk tales with the script printed on the back of each one. These were inserted into a wooden frame mounted on the back of his bicycle where everyone could see them. Moving from one picture to the next, he recited the story with gusto to the little group of children who hung onto his words. After the story, he brought out his store of candy which found a ready market among the audience. Needless to say, this type of entertainment has been made obsolete by television. But it is still used as a teaching device in school and Sunday school. Often children draw the pictures and create their own "kami shibai" as a learning project.

The plaintive music of the noodle peddler played on a small horn enticed the students poring over their books late at night. Those who felt the need of a break would come to the door and give him an order. In a few minutes he would come back, pedaling furiously through the traffic while balancing on the palm of one upraised hand the shallow tray bearing the bowls of hot noodles, then slip from his bicycle seat with the grace of a ballet dancer and make his delivery. Alas, the picturesque ballet-like noodle vender has been replaced by a box hanging from sturdy springs fastened to the back of the bicycle or motor scooter--not so colorful, but safer. You can still hear the plaintive melody, but now from a tape, and something seems to be missing.

At twilight a kind of mobile diner that I called "fly by night noodle shops" were wheeled onto the downtown streets to set up shop. These covered carts containing all the equipment needed for their restaurant could be wheeled into some back alley during the day. A kind of half curtain hung down at the front to give the illusion of privacy. Then a narrow counter was set in place, flanked by a few stools for customers. They used small charcoal-burning "shichirins" which I have described before to heat the noodles. In later years, these have been replaced by small, propane gas hot plates, for which they carry a small tank of gas. I presume they paid a small fee for their place on the street, but whether any inspection was required, or whether they were tolerated as a source of cheap nourishment, I never knew.

Various traveling repairmen who offered such services as repairing umbrellas or sharpening knives could often he heard in the daytime. Each one had a distinctive call which could be easily recognized. In these more affluent times, there are fewer of these peddlers who go from door to door, though it is still possible to have food delivered to the door. One service I read about recently in the New York Times is the bank clerk who comes monthly on his motor scooter to collect people's savings after payday. This may help to explain the high savings rates of Japanese people.

8.   Lifestyles of Missionaries

During our orientation, I had heard about the tension which often occurred between the pre-war missionaries and the "gung ho" short-term missionaries about life styles. Although the short-termers hoped to live in Japanese style houses, they were assigned to large pre-war mission houses. These were built in Western style with beds instead of "futon" on the floor, and tables and chairs instead of low tables on "tatami" (woven matting) floors with floor cushions to sit on. Some of them had rebelled against living in a big mission house and they had managed to live in the home of a Japanese family.

I found that I would be living in a newly-built Western style mission house just beside the high school and junior high buildings which had been built after the war.   The other residents, Andy and Mary, were both nearing retirement age. Andy had spent almost her whole career in the Girls' School in Hiroshima.   She had stayed through the years when Japan-American tension became so severe that she realized she was endangering her Japanese friends who tried to protect her. The "thought police" began to follow her almost daily--even when she walked over to the park at noon for quiet meditation in those stressful times.   Just a few months before Pearl Harbor, she finally obeyed the government request for foreigners to go back to their own country. During the war years, she served in the so-called "evacuation camps" in the American West, teaching young people, and interpreting for those whose English was limited. She was one of the earliest missionaries to be allowed to return during the Occupation years. After teaching a short time in Yokohama, she was allowed to come back to her beloved Hiroshima.   I appreciated Andy's concern for our household workers. She guarded their days off, and she saw to it that they did not have to work too late when we entertained guests. She was very frugal in her personal life, wearing the same clothes for many years. She didn't even spend money on a haircut, as one of her Japanese friends always cut it for her at home. When she died, she left various funds to take care of scholarships for students who would not otherwise have gone to college.

Mary, who had served many years as a chemistry teacher in Tientsin, China, was very different from Andy. She was interested in working on the interior decoration of our house. She thought we deserved to have such things as a really good Chinese rug on our living room which she managed to find, instead of a cheaper one which Andy thought would be good enough. She loved to cook and to entertain. Once a month or so, she would spend most of the day in the kitchen helping our cook to produce a real Chinese feast. Although her spoken Japanese was quite limited, she managed to shop for things she needed by using gestures when she didn't know the words. Being able to understand the meaning of Chinese characters was a help to her in reading signs.

The fourth member, Joy, with whom I had shared our orientation in Hartford, was assigned as a home economics teacher at our college. Miss Hirose asked her to start a home management house where she would teach the students Western style cooking and give them practice in running a household. Although she was about ten years younger than I was, we had a lot in common because of our recent training. When some of the ways of the older missionaries frustrated us, we could comfort each other privately. We had heard that some of the first J-3's had left big mission houses to live in Japanese style houses, sometimes with a Japanese family or a colleague. But the housing shortage was still so severe, that it was hard to find alternative places to live. Neither Joy nor I were the revolutionary type who wanted to make waves. So we tried to make the best of our situation.

We wondered if the early missionary houses had been influenced by British customs, as they tended to be very formal. One thing that irked us was when Andy would ring a little bell to let the cook know we needed something, even though we were within speaking distance of the kitchen. We didn't think we needed two helpers. But they told us the older woman who had been the pre-war helper insisted she needed her daughter to help with cleaning and other household chores. Her daughter's husband had been killed in the war, and we realized she needed a job. We found that one of the ways of dealing with their over-population was to hire two workers where one would have been enough. We noticed when we asked for a plumber, they sent two men to do the job even though it seemed that one of them just looked on. This was at a time before industry had made such a comeback providing many good jobs. We came to love and respect the two women who worked in our household, as they worked hard and were scrupulously honest in handling our money and making household decisions.

Another thing we talked about was the frequent criticism of Japanese ways of doing things. To us it smacked of condescension and racism. Eventually I came to see that we tended to look at everything through rose-colored glasses. We wanted to like everything about Japan and to become a part of their life. It might be compared to the relationship between husband and wife. After they have lived together long enough, they can see each other's weak points. So they feel free to be critical at times even though they love each other. Joy and I were like brides on a honeymoon with the Japanese people, our groom. We could see no faults in them. We saw only the good things. Actually Andy who had dedicated the best years of her life to serving in Japan, had a deep love of the Japanese people.

Since Mary Bedell had lived in China so long, she tended to compare everything in Japan to China. She preferred Chinese food to Japanese. Naturally she couldn't help having some feeling against the Japanese soldiers who had invaded China and caused so much suffering among the people there. Mary did come to love the Japanese students, and she did her best to contribute to the school in ways that were possible without knowing the language well. It was frustrating for her to teach English conversation, as she was a good chemistry teacher. But by that time there were enough good science teachers in Japan. I could understand how she found it hard to get used to a situation where she couldn't take part in making decisions as she had been able to do in China. I experienced some of that feeling myself. Even though I attended bimonthly teachers' meetings, I had no idea what they were discussing, until someone explained it afterward. Still I felt it was important to attend in order to let the other teachers know I wanted to be part of the faculty.

Joy and I often talked about how we would love to live in a Japanese style house where we wouldn't feel so different from our neighbors. But we were really surprised when an opportunity came some time in February of 1953 after our arrival in October. A Japanese house which had been rented for the two missionaries from Korea while they waited out the emergency, had been leased until May. But as the war wound down, they were allowed to go back to Korea. Thus their rented house had about three more months of the lease still left. When the older missionaries asked if Joy and I would be willing to live there for a few months to keep the house from being empty, we jumped at the chance.

This house was fairly close to our college where Joy taught, but it was about 2 miles away from our high school campus where I taught. It was a fairly large house surrounded by a beautiful hedge instead of the concrete walls which many houses had. There were lovely bushes in the small garden, and the neighborhood was rather quiet with narrow streets like a rural area. We started this new chapter in our lives full of eagerness to become a part of the Japanese community. I had to board a crowded bus every morning to go to the high school. That enabled me to feel I was experiencing the same daily struggle our Japanese teachers did every day. I also had to take my "obento" (box lunch) each day and that gave me a chance to eat in the teachers' room with the other teachers.

All the rooms in this house had "tatami" floors, but we did have beds set up in our bedrooms, and we had a space heater in one room. We soon found this oil-burning stove didn't heat up the rooms very well. No matter how early we got up to turn it on, the room was still icy by the time we were ready to get dressed. I concluded Japanese architecture had been designed by people who came from the South Sea area rather than those who came from Korea or China. Two sides of the house had sliding doors for walls that could open up in summer, allowing the breezes to blow through. Unfortunately in winter the breezes continued to blow through even when the doors were closed.

In our dining room we had a small "hibachi". It did give some warmth to our hands, but it was not meant to heat the room. The only time we really felt warm was after soaking in our Japanese bath. Then there was a wonderful heating device to use in bed, called a "yutampo". It was an oval shaped metal container with a place to unscrew at the end where hot water could be poured into it. The surface was like a corrugated roof, and somehow those curves made the water stay hot all night. Of course there was some danger of skin burns from the hot metal. That is why we enclosed it in a flannel drawstring bag in order to use it as a hot water bottle to warm up the sheets. In addition to keeping our feet warm all night, the water was still warm enough in the morning to use for washing up. Since we had no instant hot water heaters at that time, this was a real convenience.

Winters in Hiroshima were mild enough that we could manage to shiver through them by wearing many layers of clothing. It rarely got down to freezing, but the damp cold penetrated to the bone, and often it was as cold inside the house as outside.

Soon after we settled into our new house, we were asked to take in two college girls from the country who had applied too late to enter the dormitory. Schools start at the beginning of April. So by that time we had endured the worst of the cold months. This is what I wrote about the arrival of the students:

> "When I arrived home and saw the baggage of Sasaki-San which had been deposited in our entry way, I couldn't help thinking of the vast difference in the equipment of a college girl here, and that of an American co-ed. She brought a couple of big containers of charcoal. They wrap it in a straw mat with a wire frame to make it rigid. In addition she brought a hundred pound bag of rice; heavy futon for bedding which were folded and enclosed in a straw basket container; a small clay pot stove in which charcoal is burned; a low bookcase; and several 'furoshiki' (pretty squares of cloth

used to wrap everything) full of her personal belongings."

Our arrangement was to let the girls get their own meals, but we asked them to bring their food to the table to eat with us. Since we had another very young girl working for us, our house was something like a college dormitory with lots of laughter and singing when the girls got together in the evening. Since none of them spoke English, it was very good practice for us to have to get our ideas across in Japanese. The first night our young maid, Hiroko San, worked for us, she wanted to tell us that the water was hot for our bath. She consulted her dictionary and finally emerged triumphantly with just one word, "Bathroom." Whenever we had difficulty expressing our ideas, she would get out her dictionary, and we would get ours, finally coming up with the necessary words. My letter continued with this description:

> "You would have laughed to see us at the table saying again and again, 'Would you like some tea?', and 'I'm glad you liked it', and a few other phrases which they worked hard to master. Once I heard the girls practicing the phrases with each other. After each one, they would go into gales of laughter, as they were self-conscious speaking to each other in a foreign language. It was fun to introduce them to toasted marshmallows (which we could do over the hibachi), and popcorn, which was also new to them."

We agreed to eat a Japanese breakfast one morning, and serve them an American breakfast the next morning before we broke up our household. Their menu seemed a bit strange, but it was really very tasty: Bamboo shoots, green peas in the pod, a big bowl of rice, a bowl of bean curd soup, soy sauce, and a cup of green tea. It took them about two hours to prepare it. The next morning we prepared pancakes along with maple syrup which I had received from Vermont. They seemed to like it.

When the lease to our rented house ran out in May, Joy and I moved back to the mission house. Although we had really enjoyed our picturesque Japanese house, I have to admit we enjoyed being warmer the next winter. It was about fifteen years later before I had another chance to live in a real Japanese house when I was assigned to do pioneer evangelism in one of the nearby suburbs.

9. My First Summer

Although our brief interlude of living in a Japanese house had been a real adventure, I had to admit that in many ways I enjoyed the comfort of our Western style house. But it did make me feel isolated from the Japanese community around me. So in addition to the frustration of not being able to understand the language, I wanted to find more ways to become a part of the real life of the Japanese people. Soon after I arrived, another pre-war missionary came to teach in our college English department. Mary Finch, originally from Virginia, had been one of the early missionary teachers in our school while our founder, Miss Gaines, was still alive. When she returned after the war, she had been appointed to teach in another girls' school in Fukuoka, on the island of Kyushu. But she had always hoped to get back to Hiroshima where she had many friends among the Japanese people. Miss Hirose was pleased to have her join the faculty, as she had good memories of her from the pre-war years. She told me that Miss Finch's Japanese was especially polite and that she understood how to relate to the parents of our students because of her deep appreciation of Japanese customs. She was an excellent scholar in English and American literature who would enhance our college faculty which they were slowly rebuilding in the post-war years.

It was Mary Finch's idea that Joy and I might want to join her in volunteering for a high school Christian work camp which was to be held at an orphanage not far from our school that first summer. This was being sponsored by the United Church of Christ in Japan as a national project. For two weeks the young people along with a Japanese leader, would live in the orphanage and create a volley ball court to be used by the children. In the summer many of the orphans left during the school vacation if they had any relatives willing to share their home. So we could use their bedrooms. Joy and I welcomed the chance to be a part of such a project. It would enable us to be a real part of the

Japanese community and to share some of the hardships that many people were experiencing at that time.

Having Mary Finch there gave us a feeling of security, as she could speak and understand Japanese so well that she could interpret for us when needed. Also I appreciated her suggesting that each of us take one night off a week to return to the mission house for a good night's sleep and a nutritious meal. Sleeping on the floor and eating the meals served to the orphans did help us to escape from our ivory tower for awhile, but it was nice to go back to our good beds for one night.

This is my description of the work camp in a letter home:

"What a valuable two weeks it was for me, to live and work and worship with the twenty high school-age young people from many parts of Japan and to get acquainted with one of our local orphanages at first hand. Doing manual labor in the blazing sun, using rather primitive methods, and living without privacy in a large room with all the girls was not always pleasant, but I wouldn't give anything for the experience.

"Our project was to clean up a vacant lot and make a volley ball court for the orphanage. We used the standard procedure for dealing with rubble here, that is, to dig a huge hole and carry all the broken tiles, bricks and stones and bury them. If this material is left strewn out just under the surface of the ground, there will be sunken places whenever it rains. So--our job was to dig it up, carry it to the hole, and then take the extra dirt to make a smooth surface. We used the little round baskets slung on poles which are carried on one's shoulders, or between two people. The largest rocks were placed on a two-wheel cart pulled by some of the boys. We were always thankful when refreshment time came around, and the kitchen committee appeared carrying trays of iced tea, cookies, cold watermelon, or some other tidbit. I learned to appreciate this Japanese custom of 'oyatsu' in the middle of the morning and afternoon. The young people were wonderful workers and they were a real inspiration to me as I watched them work so willingly and steadily from 7:00 to 12:30 every morning. They developed a real group spirit and one of the most valuable things about the camp was the friendships made among the campers as well as between the campers and the orphans.

"Dad always liked to kid me about going all the way to Philadelphia to tear off wallpaper during my first work camp experience in 1936. So I knew he would probably laugh at my coming all the way to Japan to move dirt and rocks! But I really had a 'sisterly' feeling when I saw those weary looking women working on the roads after doing that work. I found out why they always had a towel around their necks or draped over their heads. It is handy to mop up the rivers of perspiration, and it provides some protection from the sun's glare.

"The work camp experience was a wonderful way to get acquainted with students, to learn the life of Japan, and to put into practice our Christian belief in service. The students patiently taught me Japanese and didn't mind correcting me when I sounded funny. I got used to undressing with no privacy--using a 'yukata' (summer kimono) for a screen; taking a bath with five or six girls; eating rice twice a day and such delicacies as sheets of black seaweed, yellow pickled radishes, and many other foods new to me. Some of the food I liked very much and some I had to shut my eyes and swallow."

The young people were very sincere in their desire to serve. I was especially glad to get to know the three or four girls from our school who were there and also a young boy from the church where I had my Bible class. This created a bond that lasted for many years. One of the students has continued to correspond with me all these years. She has visited me three times since I retired and she was my hostess when I returned for a visit.

Their method of cooking was quite different from ours. They used huge rice kettles which are built into a sort of furnace-like place with wood for fuel. Naturally the kitchen became unbearably hot with about three or four of these fires burning at every mealtime. The orphanage people looked on in amazement at our complicated method of dish washing, using lots of hot water and soap. Their method was much more simple--just to have each child wash his or her dishes under the cold water faucet and put them away. Our method was insisted on by Joy, who served as our dietitian. We hoped it would carry over when the young people went home. However, the prevailing custom was to use cold water for dishes.

I admired the students who spent a few hours each afternoon having sessions with the neighborhood children to teach them Bible stories and songs. That was one time I was glad I didn't know Japanese well enough to help. I usually collapsed after the noon meal until it was time for our daily bath.

The director of the orphanage was not a Christian, but he was a sincere, idealistic person who wanted to help the many orphans who had lost their parents in the bomb blast. After the summer was over, he welcomed us when Mary and I went over once a week to teach Christmas carols to the children. Some of our students went over on Saturday afternoons to have a Sunday school class with any of the children who were interested. We were pleased that the girls thought of doing that without any prodding from adults. Whenever any of us went over, the children greeted us like old friends. I noted that the language barrier didn't seem to bother them as they chattered away as if I could understand everything they said. At Christmas time Mary arranged for this orphanage choir to sing at the church which she attended. She even loaned them some of our school choir robes. They were very happy to be able to do this and it helped to boost their self-esteem.

Our last night at the work camp was memorable when we all went to the nearby castle grounds for a campfire service. The ancient castle of Hiroshima did not withstand the bomb, but the huge foundation stones were still there. We often went to that high spot overlooking the city for our morning watch. This is how I described our closing worship:

"As we sat there on the very spot where the ancient fortress of the feudal lords had been, and looked out over Hiroshima seeing the brilliant neon signs, its myriad lights, and signs of recovery, it made us think about the things that are eternal. The young Japanese minister spoke about the light of the world, using the campfire which lit up the night around us as a symbol. Here was a small group of Christians who had volunteered two weeks of their short summer vacation to express their Christian love in a tangible way among these orphaned children, some of whom had lost both parents in the tragedy of the atom bomb. As the pastor said, 'In spite of man's inhumanity to man the light is still shining in the darkness, and the darkness cannot put it out.' Governments rise and fall, but the things that are eternal cannot be destroyed."

In spite of the oppressive heat and the backbreaking work during that first summer, I felt very thankful for the chance to be a real part of the Japanese community and to share in the life of some of my students in such a meaningful way. We all felt a sense of accomplishment when we saw the finished volley ball court. We hoped it would contribute to the pleasure of those orphans whose lives had been so scarred by the dropping of that first atom bomb.

10. My Call

I had always expected to return to a parish in Vermont after I had served my three years in Hiroshima. But I knew the mission board left open the possibility that some of us might wish to apply as full time missionaries. Since I was in good health and had no family responsibilities in America, I did have this thought in the back of my mind. My widowed father had remarried and he was being well taken care of. I had always believed that one should have a definite call to become a missionary, and that had not happened to me. But by the time I was in my third year, I was being gently nudged by some of the older missionaries and Miss Hirose as well as other colleagues to consider returning to Japan. My Japanese teacher, Mrs. Harano, often spoke to me about returning and she indicated that I was really needed in the school.

Because of this, I began to think seriously about the future. I really prayed harder as to what the will of God was for my life. For a long time it seemed as if I received no answer to my prayers. I felt like complaining to God. "Why couldn't I receive a clear answer as I had heard many other people tell about?" Then gradually it dawned on me that even though I was praying for guidance, at the same time I was putting up a wall of resistance. Although I enjoyed the students, and I liked many things about Japan, I really longed to return to Vermont where I could speak in my own language and do the work of ministry which I had enjoyed so much. By this time I had no illusions about the difficulty of learning Japanese. I was also aware of the great difference in the way of thinking between Japanese and Americans. Although we are used to speaking frankly and stating our purpose when we meet with someone, in Japan one has to drink many cups of tea, and skirt around the issue before really finding out what the other person has in mind as to the purpose of the meeting. Another problem was my age. I was already 42 years old. I knew I would be required to study language two full years if I became a full time missionary. Was it foolhardy to think I could start a whole new career in a new language and a new culture at that age?

However, after admitting to myself that I was not praying with an open mind, I had a remarkable experience. I decided to try to take down the walls I had erected. When I began praying with an open mind, it seemed so obvious that I was being called to work in Japan. Even though I still wished to return to America, when I allowed myself to say "yes" to this call, I was filled with a feeling of serene peace and joy. I was sure the call was authentic, as it couldn't be wishful thinking. My next prayer was to help me want to return to Japan, and that was answered very quickly. So before my third year was over, I announced my decision to my family and friends and the mission board.

My year of furlough in America when I visited my family, spoke in churches, and spent a semester at Union Seminary working on my B.D., was enjoyable. But I was excited about returning to Japan after being commissioned as a full time missionary. I was eager to tackle the long haul of language study.

So it was in the small language school in Kobe where my two-year battle with the Japanese language began. Our teachers spoke only Japanese. Most of them did understand some English, but if we asked a question in English, they answered us in Japanese. I enjoyed my experience during those two years, as the fifty or so students came from various European countries as well as from America. I enjoyed the cosmopolitan city of Kobe where it was easy to do international shopping. The fellowship among all these missionaries was very enriching. The young Swedish woman who shared the class with me during those two years became a good friend, with whom I've corresponded over the years. I loved the tasty contributions of food made by Scandinavians and others at our picnics. Our classes were small enough that each of us had to do a lot of speaking. In addition they arranged for us to speak at our chapel services since this was a school with only missionaries in attendance. This is a description I wrote to my family during that first year in language school:

"After attending three classes each morning, my afternoons and evenings are mostly spent in studying by myself, as learning how to write and read in Japanese is an endless job. Just now after finishing my first exam, I am relaxing this weekend. I will probably forget half of the 200 or more characters (kanji) I had crammed into my head before the test. You probably know that Japanese writing is made up of little squares, diagonal lines, vertical lines, little dots and dashes in all sort of combinations. But there really is a system to it. I'm glad to say it has become interesting now instead of frustrating as it was when I first approached it."

My two years of language school passed quickly. In spite of the frustration and struggle, I found it challenging. But I still decided to concentrate more on speaking than writing. Even though I knew a couple thousand characters, I realized I couldn't keep them in my head without using them everyday. Since my work was teaching English, it would be difficult to spend enough time to remember all those unless I spent almost full time working on them. I was able to read the Bible, since the phonetic alphabet was inserted over the kanji in most Bibles. It helped also that I knew the meaning to begin with, and to have an English translation available.

When I needed to prepare a speech, I wrote it out in Romanized letters (Romaji). That made it easier for me as I could type it on my typewriter. Nowadays the language schools don't allow students to use Romaji as we did in "book one" in our language course. They begin immediately writing words in the phonetic alphabet (kana) which is a simplified form of kanji. The difference is that each kana character has only one sound, whereas the kanji indicates a word instead of a sound. Then gradually they add the Chinese characters as they learn them. They think using Roman letters becomes a crutch that is hard to give up. That is what happened to me. I felt more secure reading a manuscript in Romaji than trying to decipher the kanji and read it at natural speed.

When I finished the two years of study, it was time to think about an appointment. Our mission board allowed us some leeway in deciding where we would like to serve, after suggesting places where someone was needed. My dream had been to embark on some direct work with churches instead of teaching English. But I still felt rather insecure about taking on work where I would have to operate wholly in Japanese. Miss Hirose strongly urged me to come back to our school in Hiroshima. She assured me I could do more than teach English. I could work with students and alumnae in small groups, as well as cooperating with local churches to help them improve their church schools. I found it very hard to refuse Miss Hirose. She made it sound as if I could have a wholly different role than I had before. So, in the fall of 1958 I returned to live in the same mission house in Hiroshima. By that time Andy had returned to America with terminal cancer. But Mary Bedell, Mary Finch and Mary McMillan were still there. Mary Finch was living in an apartment at the college dormitory, and Mary McMillan had always lived in Ushita with a Japanese family. We still had a succession of J-3's who came to teach English and lived in the mission house.

With fewer hours of teaching English in the curriculum, I arranged to have more after-school Bible classes. I had one in Japanese with the junior high girls which I felt was worth while. I enjoyed being able to do it without an interpreter. They were good at dramatizing the stories, and for some of them the Bible was still new enough to be read with suspense. I also started a Saturday evening Bible class for young working girls and some of the dormitory students who were eager to learn more about the Bible.

There was one other missionary, Lois Cooper, a long time music teacher who was nearing retirement. She lived in the small prefab house next door to us where she taught piano lessons to small children. Her young maid, Myoko San, appealed to me to start a Bible class for women workers on our campus. She was an orphan whose mother had deserted her as a child. She had become a Christian after coming to work on our campus. She told me the unhappy story of our new cook at the dormitory beside our house. Her taxi-driver husband had left her for another woman and had taken her two children away from her. She had done heavy farm work until our dormitory matron had discovered her. She was an excellent cook and everyone liked her. Myoko San felt she needed a strong Christian faith to sustain her. She pointed out that many of those who worked on our campus had no chance to hear the Christian message which we were trying to teach our students. When I agreed to start such a class, she found three others who wanted to join this weekly group. At that time our main cook who had served Miss Gaines, had retired to live with her son, and her daughter had become our main housekeeper. She had been attending church with Mary Finch for awhile, and she seemed to be interested in knowing more about the Bible. There was also the wife of our janitor who lived in a small house on campus. The other one was the widowed older sister of Miss Hirose who came to be her housekeeper when she moved into the president's house on our campus.

Mrs. Harano had agreed to come to my house every Friday to help me work out my Japanese speeches and Bible lessons. Myoko San was very helpful in the class as she could answer some of their questions. In addition to our study sessions, we took time to have some fun and recreation at holiday times. Once I took them on a tour of the college campus which they had never seen, even though it was just two miles away from our high school.

This was one of my success stories, as all four of those women were eventually baptized and became members of nearby Nagarekawa Church. That happened after I had gone home on furlough. The churches had a citywide evangelistic meeting which gave them the push they needed to make the commitment. Fortunately the dormitory cook did find her son and daughter who had been placed in local orphanages. Although their father had tried to prejudice them against their mother, she was able to win them back. The young daughter came to live with her in our dormitory. She attended church with her mother and also became a Christian. She was able to get a scholarship to attend Seiwa College to study kindergarten teacher training. When she graduated, she got a job as a teacher in the Nagarekawa Church weekday kindergarten. In later years, after the young son had graduated, he had a good job. When he built a new house, he provided a room for his mother so she had a place to live after she retired. After she had lived through so much unhappiness, it was rewarding for all of us to see her reunited with her children, and to have the promise of a comfortable retirement. In spite of some of these good experiences, I didn't think I would be satisfied to spend the rest of my career in the school. I still hoped that when my Japanese was better I would be able to do some more direct work with churches. But as yet I didn't have a clear picture of what that work might be. I hoped to be able to use my Christian education training to make an improvement in the Sunday Schools. But I wasn't sure that the pastors felt a need of this kind of work.

11. School Trip

During my second year I was delighted to be offered a chance to accompany the junior class on their school trip. It is considered part of their educational curriculum to take a fairly extensive trip once in junior high and once in high school. They made monthly payments before the trip to accumulate the funds so that everyone could go. I reported in a letter to my family:

> "If you want to travel cheaply, cover a lot of ground, and be guaranteed that you'll never find yourself alone--then just go on a school trip in Japan. One by-product will be getting rid of any false modesty you might have had left over from that strange American idea that one must be alone to get undressed or to take a bath."

There were about 150 students and about 6 Japanese teachers. I was very glad that Myoko San, the young woman who worked for Lois Cooper, our music missionary, decided to go along also. I think she felt that I might need someone to look after me, since I was so new to the customs and had not yet become fluent in the language. The trip included about 40 hours of train travel, 10 hours or so on buses, plus a boat ride across a scenic lake. In Tokyo we went to a "Kabuki" show, and a grand opera. I reported that the total cost came to about $19 which included four nights in lovely Japanese inns and all our meals. At that time the exchange rate made the dollar worth a great deal when changed into yen.

As I wasn't used to their custom of such grand send-offs at the train station, I was amazed to see how many people had come to the station in Hiroshima to see us off. By the looks of the mob of parents, students, and teachers, you would have thought we were going on a round-the-world tour. A few of the girls shed real tears as they tore themselves away from their family for these few days. We had a special train just for students which we shared with two or three other schools. Each coach was made festive with red and white crepe paper streamers and the speakers played lively music as we left the station with all the people waving at us until we were out of sight. The main occupation of the girls after we left the station was munching on the various goodies each one had brought along. One of the favorite sweets at that time was wrapped caramels which they called "kyarameru," an example of an English word which had been Japanized.

When it was time for supper, I was presented with an elaborate "obento," a lunch packed in a disposable plywood box with chopsticks attached. One of the more affluent parents, probably the proprietor of a restaurant, had furnished these for all the teachers. Everyone received an "obento", but it seemed that the ones for the teachers were special. At one of the stops near our mealtime, steaming kettles of hot tea were brought on the train to fill all our cups.

When it was bedtime, I discovered their clever method for getting a good night's sleep on a coach. Each pair of the double facing seats was furnished with boards cut to the right size to support a person between the seats. The other possibility was to use the board for a slanting back support and stretch out on one seat. The problem was that my legs were too long to be comfortable using either method. Japanese travelers are always equipped with handy little clean-up kits containing washcloth, soap and toilet articles. In preparation for the night, each girl had a good wash-up; then they took off their dresses and proceeded to put on flannel pajamas over the rest of their clothing. After that they curled up for a good night's rest. The two teachers who sat beside me, arranged their coats and small blanket over them, unrolled their long underwear which they kept rolled above their hose in daytime, and went soundly to sleep. When I woke up every few hours feeling as if my neck was out of joint, and my legs doubled up to stay, I cast envious looks at their peaceful slumbers.

Next morning when we got off at a city near Tokyo and boarded four big buses, I discovered the system which made it easy to handle so many students. They divided them into five groups with a student leader for each one. When the teacher blew his whistle, they lined up in groups, and each leader checked the names to see if everyone was there. Then they received instructions as to what came next. I couldn't help remembering what a big responsibility we thought it was when about four of us adults led 16 of the young people in our church youth fellowship on a trip from Vermont to New York. Of course one difference is that Japanese students are used to being regimented from kindergarten on up as they always have such large numbers in each class.

To our disappointment it rained all day making it impossible to see the lovely mountain scenery during our long bus trip. At one place there was a lookout where we were supposed to see into ten "countries" as the different sections were characterized in feudal times. I felt we were lucky to reach the top without an accident considering the deep snow which we encountered as we went up those narrow twisting roads. Of course we just had to imagine what the view would have been on a sunny day. Our boat ride across Hakone Lake was still shrouded in rain and clouds. When another bus took us through a volcanic area, we could see and smell the sulfurous vapor rising from the many hot springs. Our only entertainment that evening was taking baths in the famous sulfur water "ofuro" (Japanese bath) which was supposed to be good for all kinds of ailments. Four of us teachers were in a "honeymoon suite', which contained several rooms opening on a lovely garden. I reported that the regular cost would have been $10 a night which seemed like a large amount at that time.

Japanese inns are always attractive and the maids do everything for your comfort. First you remove your shoes which are placed in a locker. Then they take you to your "tatami" room which becomes both your dining room and bedroom during your stay. There is always a lovely flower arrangement in the alcove known as the "tokunoma." There is no furniture except a low table in the middle and thin floor cushions to sit on. Immediately they serve green tea and some kind of sweet cakes. Then at meal time, they bring in extra tables and serve your meal. The expected procedure is to take a bath soon after arrival, and then put on the cotton kimono and the heavy quilted outer kimono provided by the hotel. It is perfectly proper to appear in this outfit to visit with friends or to take walks outdoors.

Most of the time we six women teachers slept in one large room. But the men teachers, the photographer (no important occasion is complete without him), and the travel bureau man usually ate with us in our room. That was why I felt rather insecure about getting undressed, though the men usually went to their own room by the time the maids brought out the bedding. Having always lived in a crowded country makes them have a different kind of modesty from ours. I found that any Japanese woman knows how to get undressed with only a hotel kimono as a curtain. They are so skillful that you wonder just when they got out of their clothes.

As for food, we usually had elaborate dinners at night. There would be lots of rice which the maids dished out of the large lacquer pot into our individual rice bowls. There would be bits of cooked fish, cooked meat, vegetables, and some kind of green salad. The greatest delicacy was the "sashimi" -- the pretty slices of pink raw fish to be dipped in soy sauce with a bit of horseradish. I have to admit that I had a psychological block about eating the raw fish. So I usually passed it over to my next door neighbor. But the first night I was trying hard to fit in with all the Japanese customs. So I ate a little of it. The meal ended with a lacquer bowl of clear soup and of course many cups of green tea. Before we went to bed, the teachers asked me if I would prefer toast and a Western breakfast the next morning. But I was very scornful of that idea, insisting that I would eat the traditional breakfast along with them. To my chagrin, I woke up feeling nauseated the next morning and I just couldn't face that breakfast! I couldn't help wondering if it was because of the raw fish! My brother, Neil, had warned me that the Japanese breakfast was the hardest meal to get used to. They served paper thin sheets of black seaweed which has a fishy taste, a raw egg, bits of cold spinach and pickles made of the large "daikon" radishes, tiny whole fish and a cloudy soup made of fermented beans. Of course there was lots of rice and tea. I made out all right by mixing the raw egg with my rice. Most of the Japanese mixed the raw egg with soy sauce into which they dipped the seaweed.   That certainly didn't appeal to me.   The most astounding dish that was ever served during the trip was something that looked like white worms, but I found it was quite good, with the taste of lobster.   Our noon meal was always an "obento" which, I had to admit, was more creative than our sandwiches.   The rectangular wooden box was packed tight with cooked rice, with small compartments at one end for bits of cooked fish or meat, vegetables and pickles and sometimes fruit. It was always decorated with some kind of greenery, often artificial palm leaves.   I found the lunches to be pretty good, but I did get rather tired of having to face one of those lunch boxes every day at noon.   Having cold rice was hard for me to get used to.

The highlight of our two days in Tokyo was the "kabuki," the ancient Japanese drama which is performed with such lavish costumes and scenery.   I found it fascinating even though I couldn't understand the language.   Once I turned to the student who was with me and asked what the actor had said.   She replied, "Sensei, just look at it and don't worry about the words. I don't understand it either."

Actually some of the dialogue is in old Japanese which is hard for young people to understand.   She was one of the students who had shared the work camp with me. and she could understand a good deal of English.   She was very helpful to me as an interpreter when I needed one.   The play began at 5:00 PM and ended at 10:00 PM.   Everyone ate supper during the long interlude.   The theater was truly luxurious with various restaurants and bars located around the auditorium.   Of the three plays that night, I enjoyed the comedy the best, since the actions told the story without any need of language.

That night, after we returned to the hotel, everything happened. Though it was already late, we had to sit down and drink tea with several visitors who came to see us.   Everybody's friends and relatives in Tokyo looked us up.   Our room was just like Grand Central Station.   I saw there was no hope of getting undressed before midnight.   Then as the climax, two students came into our room, half carrying one of the girls.   They said she seemed to be sick, and just as they reached the threshold, the girl collapsed in a dead faint. We managed to get her on one of the futons, and everyone began rubbing her arms and legs. She looked so purple and her heart beat was so weak, that the teachers were quite frightened. By the time they managed to get a doctor, she had come round and seemed to be quite normal. The doctor said it was a mild heart attack. The girl did have a weak heart, and that strenuous day had been too much for her. The doctor suggested she stay in the hotel the next day instead of going sight-seeing. After they got her settled for the night--still in our room--and calmed the girl friend who sobbed uncontrollably when it was all over, the teachers started for their nightly bath, even though it was 1:00 AM. I was half asleep between my bed quilts when they returned, but I noticed they sat down and had a leisurely cup of tea before they finally turned off the light at about 2:00 AM. The sad part was that we had to get up at 5:00 the next morning.

That early morning start was for our trip to Nikko, a famous scenic resort which they call the "Switzerland of Japan." It is high up in the mountains and the scenery reminded me of Vermont. It is famous for the highly decorated shrines built in memory of a famous warrior who once ruled that section of the country. The narrow road leading to the shrines is lined with majestic trees which are related to our redwoods in California. Later we ascended the mountain on a cable car that took us straight up and came out at a beautiful mountain lake. In spite of the beauty, it was hard for me to appreciate the place because of the bitter cold. It was like Vermont in early March. The temperature was about zero, and there was no heat in our hotel except a few pieces of smoldering charcoal in the "hibachi." The faucets were all frozen solid. But somehow they had managed to fill the large bath with water so everyone could have a bath before going to bed. We had to wait for the maids to put out the bedding. So we sat around the "hibachi" and sang songs in order to forget how cold we were. The students were much more stoical than I was. My friend, Myoko San, did her best to help me get warm. She led me on a walk around the room in order to get my circulation going. All I wanted to do was to jump into bed where I might get warmed up. I had contracted a heavy cold, and I thought it best not to take a hot bath. Instead, I soaked my feet in the hot water to try to warm them up and then dived into the pile of heavy quilts where I felt warm for the first time that day.

Our last morning in Tokyo included an hour's stop in a big department store. Every girl emerged loaded with "omiyage," the presents one is expected to take home to sisters, brothers, and cousins and grandparents. I got into the mood and bought some small gifts to take to the children of the friends where I planned to visit. My old friend from our Cedarville Sunday Night Club, Frances Bray, had invited me to spend a week with them in Kobe to rest up after the trip before heading back to Tokyo for our annual missionary conference. Of course I had to buy gifts for their maid and also for our two helpers in Hiroshima. By noon we were ready to board our special train which had been waiting on a siding at the station. Quite a few people came to see us off. There were relatives, friends, former pupils of one teacher who had once taught in Tokyo, and the leader of that work camp I took part in the summer before. He knew me and several of the students on the trip. All these people brought some present, usually something to eat on the train such as fruit or candy or cakes.

We had one more night of sleeping on our little boards. When daylight came, and we stopped at a big station, I discovered why they have those long sinks with mirrors over them on all the station platforms. The girls went out--some still in their pajamas--and took their little clean-up kits. They turned on the faucets and splashed water on their hands and faces and had a good wash-up. Then they proceeded to brush their teeth--all this right on the platform in the train station. They came back on the train looking very fresh and then they put on their unwrinkled dresses which had been carefully folded up the night before.

I was thankful I could get off at Osaka instead of going all the way back to Hiroshima which would have taken another half day. I had come to feel quite at home on that train, though. I began to understand something of the secure feeling which

Japanese students feel from always being part of a group. Though this sounds like a strenuous trip, it didn't seem that way because everything was taken care of. There was always a bus or train ready to whisk us away. We didn't have to worry about making any travel arrangements. It was a good opportunity for me to get better acquainted with the teachers and some of the students. After saying my thank you speech to the travel bureau man, the photographer, and the teachers (Myoko San had coached me as to what to say), I got off the train and took the local electric train which arrived at the Brays in time for me to feast on hot coffee, toast, eggs and bacon. By that time I had a new appreciation for a real American breakfast!

12. Background Of The School

Before I went to Japan, I knew very little about the history of mission work in that land, although I had occasionally heard Japan missionaries speak. I found that even though the Hiroshima Girls' School had been destroyed by the atom bomb, its history and tradition were very much alive. Mission work in Japan never progressed in a straight line, but rather it had experienced drastic swings of the pendulum from favorable to hostile reception by the people. The earliest Christian missionaries had come from Portugal. The great Catholic missionary, Francis Xavier, went to Japan in the 1500's where he had unusual success in converting many people to Christianity. He persuaded the leaders of that feudal society to embrace Catholicism, and it naturally followed that those samurai, who were loyal to their lord, would become Christians. But when the Shogun rulers saw what was happening, they feared that Japan would come under the domination of Spain or Portugal as other Asian countries had done. They had heard that the missionaries came first, and then the military people followed to colonize the country for their own profit.

Their solution was to ban Christian missionaries and to have a campaign to force all Japanese Christians to renounce their faith or suffer imprisonment or death. They even crucified some of the Christians who refused to recant their faith. In Nagasaki which had become the center of Catholicism, there is a moving monument to twelve Christians who suffered crucifixion rather than renounce their faith. Christians were told they must recant their faith by stepping on the "fumie" which bore the image of Jesus or the Virgin Mary, or else suffer death. Many Christians were willing to renounce their faith, or at least to go through the outward ceremony. But it was discovered three hundred years later that many of the Christians went underground and continued as "hidden Christians" even without benefit of ordained priests.

It was that determination to ban Christianity that caused the Tokugawa rulers to decree that no foreigners could enter their country, and no Japanese could go abroad. Of course there were exceptions such as the young man, Niijima Jo, who had managed to get a Bible in Chinese and was determined to find out more about that forbidden religion. He escaped from Japan by boarding a ship which took him to Boston where a Christian sea captain treated him as a son. The young man eventually graduated from Amherst College where he became a strong Christian. Then he went back to Japan and founded Doshisha University as a Christian college in Kyoto.

For 200 years the Japanese people were totally isolated from the Western world until Commodore Matthew Perry sailed his "black ships"--as they were called in Japan--into Tokyo Bay in July of 1853. Although initially there was a slogan "Expel the barbarians," eventually they knew they had to bow to a superior force. In spite of a certain amount of fighting among the feudal lords, this marked the end of the rule of the Shoguns. Then came the restoration of the Emperor known as the Meiji Revolution in 1868. It is hard to imagine what it must have been like for those who lived through the Meiji Revolution which initiated one of those drastic swings of the pendulum in Japanese history. Charles Iglehart describes it thus:

> "The blow struck Japan like a tidal wave, and soon the dikes of seclusion were down and the nation itself was launched on the unruly waters of modern life." [1]

As the people realized how much they had missed during the long period of isolation, they were eager to absorb as much as they could of Western culture. Under government sponsorship, young men went abroad to study Western science, government, education, and court systems. Japanese men began to wear Western suits, after they realized how strange their long flowing kimonos and wooden clogs looked in London, Paris and New York.

---

[1] "A Century of Protestant Christianity in Japan"—Charles W. Iglehart, p. 26

After the treaty of 1859 was signed, American and European churches sent missionaries to explore the possibilities. At first they were restricted to certain areas around the seaports. It was not until 1873 that the so-called "proscription boards" all over Japan were taken down. These had proclaimed that Christians were not allowed in Japan, and that anyone confessing Christianity would be put to death. Naturally missionaries found it hard to make converts in such a hostile atmosphere. But they used their time to learn the language and to begin translating the Bible.

One of the earliest Protestant missionaries, Dr. James C. Hepburn, was a medical doctor whose clinic attracted many people. At a time when direct evangelism was almost impossible, he gained the trust of people who appreciated his medical skills. He also found time to work out a Romanized system of writing Japanese to make it easier for foreigners to read and write the spoken language. It is still known as the Hepburn system. Other early missionaries worked on Japanese-English dictionaries and they made a translation of the Bible with the help of Japanese scholars. Today's Japanese Bibles have been translated from the original Greek and Hebrew by competent Japanese Christian scholars.

Many of the missionaries believed the best way to introduce the Christian faith was by means of schools where young people could study the Bible and be introduced to Christian beliefs. Since there had been no widespread education for girls except among the elite classes, women missionaries started schools for girls. Some schools for boys were also founded, but there were not so many as for girls.

The founding of the Hiroshima Girls' School where I was appointed was such a school. A young man named Sunamoto was a sailor on a Japanese ship which went to California. While he had time on shore leave, he attended a meeting at Dr. Gibson's mission for Japanese in San Francisco. He heard the Christian message as a call to adventure greater than his call to the sea. He became an enthusiastic Christian and he wanted to share his new faith with his mother. When he went back home, he decided to start a school for young women. He believed that if the young women of Japan could become Christian their influence would be strong enough to bring their children into the faith.

Already the Methodist Church South had sent missionaries to Kobe to start a Christian school. One of those was a China-born missionary, Dr. J. W. Lambuth and later his son, Walter Lambuth, who had left their work in China to evangelize in Japan. They had all they could do to continue their work in Kobe. But when Mr. Sunamoto appealed to them to send a young woman to help start a Christian school for girls, they felt this was a Macedonian call such as St. Paul received in the biblical account. They wrote to the Methodist bishop in America where an appeal was sent out in their church paper for a qualified teacher to help start a school in Hiroshima. Miss Nannie B. Gaines, a young teacher from Kentucky, then teaching in Florida, was the only one who answered the ad. After a long wait when she had almost given up, a letter arrived telling her she had been accepted by the Mission Board to serve in the newly opened girls' school in Hiroshima. Within four days she was "speeding across the American continent for San Francisco to embark for the Orient." [2] So, in 1887, after a long ocean voyage, she arrived at the port of Kobe where she was met by the pioneer missionaries, the Lambuths, whom she had long admired. She arrived in time to take part in the annual missionary conference where they reported that many calls had come from Japanese communities asking for help in the study of the Bible.

She learned her first lesson in patience, while waiting for her passport for her trip to Hiroshima to be arranged. It took as long to get passports to go from Kobe to Hiroshima as it had to come from America to Japan. She felt fortunate to have the young Lambuth couple and their two children to accompany her to her lonely post in Hiroshima.

Miss Gaines wrote home about her arrival:

---

[2] "Gaines Sensei" –Samuel M. Hilburn, p. 1

"Our gallant little steamer came into Ujina, the port of Hiroshima, about sunset, the 12th of October. ...Here Sunamoto and some of the church members welcomed us. People crowded around in such numbers it was difficult to get into the jinrikisha, or for the vehicle to get through the crowd once we were in. ...The three miles from Ujina to Hiroshima, through salt marshes and paddy fields, was made in comfort with our sure-footed jinrikisha men. Reaching the little Japanese hotel, we were welcomed by the proprietor and his wife and numerous attendants, all sitting on their heels at the broad entrance. In the little rooms upstairs reserved for us we found the other church members waiting to welcome us." [3]

The next morning, messengers came asking her to come to the little school which had opened in an upstairs room over a theater, as the pupils were anxious to meet their new teacher. She was given no time for rest or for orientation, as she taught English during the morning hours and studied Japanese in the afternoon with a teacher more intent on getting English than advancing his pupil in Japanese. In addition, she taught English to boys in a night school, taught foreign sewing, and attended evening prayer meetings without understanding a word of what was said.

One of the interesting stories the older missionaries told me about Miss Gaines was a near catastrophe which happened to her baggage. With her usual foresight, she had brought a piano with her. She used her outfit allowance for new missionaries to buy it. When the piano was being taken off the small ship which brought her to the port of Hiroshima, the workmen had no idea how heavy it was, as they had no experience with pianos. As a result, they dropped it into the Bay of Hiroshima. Somehow they managed to fish it out, and I was told that it continued to be used in the school for many years. The school has always had a strong emphasis on music. Japanese young people were strongly attracted to Western hymns and oratorios. Christians often say

---

[3] Ibid. p. 39

that if the Christian faith had been as widely accepted as Christian music, there would be a majority of Christians in Japan.

When I arrived at the school, there were still quite a few Japanese people, and some missionaries, who remembered Miss Gaines during her latter years, as she stayed in Hiroshima until her death. She was a person of vision who had strong determination and real executive ability and she was always eager to learn new methods. Her commitment to evangelize the women of Japan enabled her to fight against inconceivable odds during those early years.

Just two years after the school began, there was a swing in the pendulum when Japanese reaction to Western influences set in. They started a Buddhist school for girls with the aim of giving a more traditional curriculum to counteract the new ideas from the Western world. Because of decreasing enrollment and the lack of qualified teachers, Miss Gaines was forced to close the school and go back to Kobe with the Lambuths. Some missionaries thought the day of Christian schools for girls was over. But Miss Gaines never considered giving up. While in Kobe she had time to do serious reflecting and praying about her mission. Her conclusion was to work for:

> "an education not superimposed, not involving a radical break with the long and precious heritage of the past, but building upon it so as to realize unfulfilled possibilities. She determined to build a <u>Japanese</u> school, that would prepare its students for life in the Japan of their day. She would give them Christian ideals, but she was content to let them work out their own changes in customs." [4]

The real beginning of Hiroshima Girls' School was in 1889 when a two year and a four year course were provided, with a special course for irregulars. In spite of the small number of students, and the difficulty in finding Christian teachers, Miss Gaines had reopened the school. Fortunately, Mr. Lambuth had purchased a lot for the "school that was to be." The Hongkong

---

[4] Ibid. p. 47

Shanghai Banking Corporation had agreed to lend the money without collateral because of the good name of the Lambuths which was known throughout the Far East.

She realized the day had passed when Japanese were eager to have foreign teachers. The report of the Mission Committee said, "Every inch of the ground is to be henceforth hotly contested. We must do thorough work, or no work; we must have equipment or abandon the field." [5]

Miss Gaines believed that a new building was essential to prove to the Japanese people that this school was really to be permanent. Without waiting for an answer from the mission board for funds, she started raising a building fund by putting up her own personal funds and inspiring other missionaries to make gifts and loans to the enterprise. By the end of July, the new building had been constructed. Although there was still hostility to Christianity, having a building increased the respect of the community for this new school.

But at the fall opening, only seven new students came to enroll. That situation changed after a year when Miss Gaines with the help of a Japanese manager was able to meet the standards of the Japanese government schools. By the spring of 1891, a primary school was constructed and by September a kindergarten building was ready to open. All this was done without asking for money from the Mission Board, as Miss Gaines mortgaged her own salary. The principal of one of the government schools had requested Miss Gaines to start a kindergarten as the only one in the city was about to close for lack of funds. Fortunately the American Board of the Congregational Church had started a kindergarten training school in Kobe. So Miss Gaines was able to get one of their first graduates and one of their teachers to come to her new one about to be opened.

However, disaster struck again when the kindergarten building was destroyed by a typhoon and a month later the new school building went up in flames. Probably many people thought that would be the end of this Christian school, but again it never

---

[5] Ibid. p. 49

occurred to Miss Gaines to give up on what she believed was her God-given task. Classes were held in a rented building. Fortunately she received an outpouring of gifts and letters to help with rebuilding. One letter was from the wife of a bishop who expressed her sympathy, and assured her they were doing all they could to secure funds for rebuilding the school. The disaster also gained a great deal of attention and sympathy among the Japanese community. Homes were offered to students and teachers. Even a Buddhist priest offered to lend desks and other equipment without remuneration.

On October 28th when she had gathered her little flock about her for vespers in their rented building, a messenger came with a cablegram from America. She was almost afraid to read it, lest there was more bad news. But it consisted of one word, "Rebuild!" There was great joy among them, and they all joined in singing the Doxology. It so happened that for once there was a surplus in the mission treasury. Dr. Lambuth had gone to America to present the cause of the Japan mission to the churches. So that helped to explain this unexpected good news. Within record time plans were made to put up three new buildings, a kindergarten, a recitation building, a chapel, and a dormitory.

In 1895, in spite of her crowded schedule, she started a kindergarten teacher training school. She had found it so difficult to find qualified teachers that she decided to do it herself. At first she taught them before breakfast and after school in her own bedroom. But eventually it became an excellent training school, which Miss Gaines considered one of her most important achievements. Later it merged with a similar training college in the Osaka area to become Seiwa Christian College for Women which is now a four year co-educational college with graduate courses for pre-school teachers and Christian education directors.

In going through the archives of our Methodist Mission Board, I found many letters which Miss Gaines regularly sent to New York. They almost always contained earnest appeals for more funds, as she had such a broad vision of what the school could become. Nearly always the answers to her letters explained why they couldn't increase the amount they were sending. At times when she believed there was a crisis demanding immediate action, she must have been frustrated to wait at least a month for her letter to reach New York, and another month for the answer to arrive, even if it was written immediately. But she didn't always wait for action from the mission board. She regularly dipped into her own meager salary to get some new work started.

By 1919 there seemed to be a swing of the pendulum which favored the Christian schools. Miss Gaines was requested by the city and prefectural authorities to add a Higher Department for training teachers in domestic science, English and music. They stated that the mission school could command the services of foreign teachers who could prepare teachers better than the government schools, especially in English and music. She realized this would require a stupendous task of expansion.

As she was nearing retirement age, and was hoping to be relieved of administrative duties to do more evangelizing among the graduates, she requested they send a man to initiate this new work which she described as a man-sized job. As I read this, I thought she was surely a "child of her time" who had been taught the limitations of women. Surely she had already accomplished a man-sized job in establishing Hiroshima Jo Gakuin. So in April of 1920 the mission board honored her request by appointing the Rev. S. A. Stewart as president and Miss Gaines as president emeritus.

13. After Miss Gaines

By the time Mr. Stewart retired, there were qualified Japanese Christian men to take over the leadership of the school. When World War II ended, Dr. Takuo Matsumoto, the president, who had received his theological education in America, had many friends there. The atom bomb fell when students and teachers were assembled for chapel. The death toll was high, but Dr. Matsumoto miraculously survived. Although he had helped his wife and daughter flee to the nearby park, where he thought they would be safe, they were drowned in the river where crowds of victims were pushing to reach the water. In spite of his loss, he made a super-human effort to rescue students who were trapped under the debris. Almost immediately he started a rebuilding program. There was no thought of discontinuing the school even though the campus had been completely destroyed.

The first Japanese president, Mr. Zensuke Hinohara, the immediate successor to Mr. Stewart, had acquired a large tract of land on a mountain in Ushita, about two miles out of the city just before the war started. Although some people thought he was foolish to buy this mountainous land which was so far away from the downtown campus, it proved to be a great asset after the war. Because of war-time restrictions on erecting buildings, they could not begin using that area right away. The only building they had put up before the war was a rambling lodge used for physical training which was supposed to build up the stamina of the young people for patriotic purposes. Fortunately that building survived the bomb. It was used as a home for the president as well as a dormitory for students right after the war. At the foot of the mountain, temporary barracks were put up for classrooms where students and teachers bravely shivered through the winter in order to continue their education.

In 1950 the Japan Bible Society asked Dr. Matsumoto to head up the committee to translate the New Testament into contemporary Japanese. As he was a New Testament scholar, well versed in Greek, he was highly qualified to work on such a translation from the original Greek to modern Japanese. Although about three new buildings had been constructed by that time, there was still an enormous task to reconstruct the two campuses.

For the first time in its history, a Japanese woman was asked to become the president and take on the huge job of helping the school rise up from the ashes. Miss Hamako Hirose was the president when I arrived. She had graduated from the school in the early part of the 20th century. The story of her life is fascinating. She told me that Miss Gaines studied the map of the prefecture with the goal of targeting some of the rural areas untouched by Christian work, in the hope of attracting students. She advertised an entrance examination for young girls in some of those country schools. Her hope was that they might go back to their villages after graduation to spread the Christian faith.

Hamako, who had a burning desire to become a teacher, persuaded her parents to let her take the examination. Her father walked with her on a cold March morning on the long trip to the school where the exam was offered. When she met him at the noon hour, she told him she thought she was doing well on the test. The next day when she talked to her teacher about some of the questions, he agreed that her answers had been correct. But to her dismay, she heard no word about the results of the test before it was time to begin public school. Her parents said she might as well make up her mind she had failed. So she reluctantly registered at the public school. In a few days, however, she was delighted to receive a letter telling her that she had indeed passed the test and was accepted at Hiroshima Girls' School. Through some error, the letter had been delayed. So her parents helped her pack up her belongings and prepared her for living in the dormitory of the Christian school.

She responded to the teaching of Christianity which she had heard for the first time, and during her years at the school, she was baptized and joined the nearby Methodist church. She proved to be one of the outstanding students who was chosen by Miss Gaines after graduation to have the offer of a scholarship to study in a small Christian college in Missouri. One of Miss Gaines' goals was to encourage the most promising students to become leaders so the school could provide its own Japanese teachers instead of relying on foreigners. Miss Hirose said it was very unusual in that period to allow a young woman to go abroad at a time when she would normally have been preparing to become a wife and mother. Her parents had come to trust Miss Gaines' judgment as to the ability of their daughter. Since she had such a strong determination to become a teacher, they gave their consent. Actually there was no fund for scholarships at that time, but one of Miss Gaines' brothers had agreed to provide the money for this promising young woman.

During her years in the American college, she received a letter from Miss Gaines telling her of her hope that some day Hamako would be able to take her place as the head of the school. Miss Hirose treasured that letter and when she became the president, she had it framed. She placed it in a prominent position in her office in the new administration building which was finished soon after I arrived at the school.

When the call came for her to take the job of president, she was serving as the president of Seiwa College in the Osaka area. She had been awarded one of the post-war Crusade Scholarships offered by the Methodist Church in America to outstanding leaders after the long years of war and deprivation. She received a doctorate in Education from Columbia University in combination with Union Seminary. Her dissertation was an extended plan for Seiwa College, but she felt she couldn't refuse the call of her alma mater. She agreed to take the position, provided she could have Miss Katherine Johnson, a pre-war missionary, to be her co-president for a few years. She realized the enormity of the task of gathering teachers and constructing buildings for the new four-year college as well as for the high school. Miss Johnson received a leave of absence from the faculty in Atlanta where she was teaching. They made an excellent team, and the new school began to rise out of the ashes. In the immediate post-war years, the Methodist churches in America contributed fairly large sums of money to rebuild the high school on the original site downtown, as well as the new college buildings on the unused site on the hillside in Ushita two miles away.

Miss Hirose continued as president until she retired in her 70's in 1974. The board of trustees asked her to stay on as chair of the board for several years after that. Although her health was beginning to deteriorate, she was able to participate in the celebration of the 100th anniversary in 1986. She made an excellent speech on that occasion. She was able to greet alumnae from many parts of the world as well as from Japan. By that time the school was supported by Japanese Christians without help from American mission boards except for one or two missionary teachers. Our school joined other mission schools in contributing money to the fund in Tokyo which helped to support missionaries from America.

That came about when the devaluation of the dollar cut the mission board budgets in half. At that time the Japan church declared their wish to take some responsibility for supporting missionaries. Because of the sudden rise in costs due to the "oil shock", there was concern that mission boards might have to send some of the missionaries home. The church in Japan felt that anyone who had a God-given call to Japan should not have to give up their work for lack of funds. They reminded everyone how churches and schools had been receiving missionaries for over 100 years without cost. Now when Japanese were more affluent, it was only right for them to help pay missionary salaries.

I think Miss Gaines would be happy to see the school as it is today. At the request of many alumnae, a kindergarten was started again after the high school and college buildings were finished. It is located on the new hillside land near the college. What was once just a wooded hillside has become a bustling housing development with many young families in new homes. They are pleased to have a kindergarten nearby. In addition, many of the graduates who live in other parts of the city gladly send their children on the school bus which picks up pupils all over town.

The college has recently added a graduate course in English in addition to the four-year college which offers majors in English, home economics, and Japanese language. They continue the tradition of good musical education. There is now a German pipe organ in the high school chapel and an electric organ in the college chapel, as well as a number of practice pianos. At the celebration of the 100th anniversary of the school, a hundred-voice choir accompanied by their orchestra filled the large city auditorium with the majestic strains of Handel's Hallelujah Chorus. They have come a long way from the music department which contained only that piano which had been fished out of Hiroshima Bay. The legacy of Miss Gaines lives on.

14. Is It A Christian School?

Because of its history, I expected that Hiroshima Jo Gakuin would have many Christians both in the student body and on the faculty. So it was a shock to discover that not all the teachers were Christian, and only a small percentage of the students were. But I began to realize that in a country where less than one percent of the population were members of Christian churches, it would be very hard to recruit enough qualified faculty members from that small segment. The president, and the heads of departments were required to be Christians as well as the board of trustees. Special scholarships were given to children of ministers' families, but since it was a private school, some children from other Christian families could not afford the tuition.

Every student was required to study one year of Bible, a class which met once a week and was taught by the school chaplain. Junior and senior high school students were required to attend chapel every morning except one day set aside for home room. Each student had her own hymnal and Bible. I wondered how much this meant to the students who had no background in Christianity. They sang the hymns beautifully, but they were sometimes rather inattentive to the speakers. Christian teachers took turns giving the brief talks, and naturally some were better than others. My feelings were mixed as to whether this school was carrying out the purpose for which it was founded. It seemed that most of the students just went through the forms without comprehending the true message of the Bible and the Christian faith. But soon after I arrived, I heard some of the English speeches given at an oratorical contest sponsored by Miss Anderson's English group. They had chosen their own subjects, and almost everyone had a Christian theme. I was thrilled to hear one of the girls say in her soft sweet voice:

"The first impression that I received when I entered this school with joy and hope was that there was a gentle and soft air among the teachers and pupils and in every inch of this school. At that time I wondered why I felt so, but today I found it out--I think I found it out--that is, this school is a Mission School. And now at the morning worship when I sing hymns and offer prayers to God quietly, my heart is warmed as I have never had such an experience as this before. And even I who had no faith till now can have faith in my heart and feel happiness and hope."

When I heard this, I felt that I had a lot to live up to as I worked and lived among these students. I hoped I could do my part to create such an atmosphere. I discovered also that among the small number of girls who had become Christians, some of them were enthusiastic about their church work. One of my students wrote this account of her work as a Sunday School teacher:

"Every Sunday I leave home at 8 o'clock and go to church. First of all I sweep our room and have worship with my friends. At 9 o'clock the children come, and I have worship with my children. My happiest time is when I sing hymns with them. It looks easy to tell Jesus' story to children and sing and pray with them. But it is rather difficult. For instance, when I am busy all the week, I cannot prepare the story for Sunday. So I study it on Saturday evening. Next day, on Sunday, I tell them the story. Even though, I, myself, think that I am doing well, they want to talk with their friends. This shows that my preparation is not enough. So I have to think and prepare the story all the week praying to God to make me stronger. When I see them listening to the story eagerly or bowing their heads, I think this is the most valuable work for me and I feel very happy. The story they like most is the one about the lost sheep. I told it to them a month ago, but even now I can remember the tears in their eyes. They listened to the story very eagerly. They never talked nor moved their heads or hands. I told them how Jesus loves us and waits for us to go back to him. I will try to be a better teacher for my children. I hope to continue this work as long as I can."

Even at the time I went to Japan, there were mixed feelings among church people as to whether we should be spending money on sending missionaries to other countries. Some people said the Japanese had their own religion and we had no right to try to preach to them about the Christian faith. In one of my early letters sent to sponsoring churches, I tried to share some of my feelings with the people in those churches:

"As I walk down the streets of Hiroshima, I am often reminded of the people back in America who do not believe in missions. I wonder if they realize we export everything else beyond our borders, and would they have us keep our religion which is the foundation of our civilization at home? On my way to church, I pass the Hiroshima Ford Motor Co. (with the same familiar Ford logo as seen in the U.S.); the headquarters of the National Cash Register Co. from Dayton, Ohio; a large theater which has a blazing sign, 'The Home of American Movies' and many others. Isn't it too bad to export the superficial elements of our civilization without the deeper values which are more important? Unfortunately many people do pick up only the worst things from our country and do not discover our basic faith in God. All the stores now display Christmas trees at Christmas as a purely commercial proposition. A couple of years ago, our leading bank had a huge tree in its lobby with all kinds of gay baubles to decorate it. When one of our young missionaries went into the bank, she was amazed to see among the decorations some bright shiny whiskey bottles. She tactfully explained to the man in charge that Christmas has a sacred meaning to Christians, and suggested that the whiskey bottles were not suitable. He apologized profusely and offered to remove them, but he was quite surprised because as he said, 'I always thought that was a part of your Christmas celebration.' Unfortunately, that is what some of the Americans in the Occupation had demonstrated in Japan."

Another young missionary had approached our largest department store to suggest using a manger scene which she provided to tell the real story of Christmas. As a result the store decorators prepared a window display with the miniature manger scene in the center, surrounded by greenery and behind it a blue background sprinkled with gold stars, with one larger than the others. An artistic scroll at one side proclaimed (in Japanese characters) "Glory to God in the highest and on earth peace, good will toward men." The store decorators had worked it out themselves, using a sketch which some of our students had drawn from a Christmas card. As I have indicated before, this was a time when Japanese people were eager to learn more about democracy and about how to make a peaceful world. During that period, there was a so called "boom" in the churches, as people had the feeling that the backbone of American democracy could be found in their Christian faith.

The Christmas season was joyfully celebrated at our school with many parties and special programs. We were invited to festive dinners followed by a lovely program at both the high school and the college dormitories. These celebrations were climaxed with the chapel service just before we closed for winter vacation. They gave it in our chapel with special lighting and scenery. A simple background of black with silver palm trees in silhouette and stars throughout the sky made an effective setting for the manger scene which the students dramatized. The Japanese kimono makes a good foundation for Palestinian costumes, and the "zori" on their feet make good sandals. Both the speaking choir and the singing choir carried lighted candles, and they wore simple white choir capes which a group of students had made with the help of one of the missionary teachers. Their voices sounded like angels, and their natural grace and rhythm made the pantomiming very lovely. The Christmas offering was sent to Korea to the missionary, Miss Cooper, who spent two years in Hiroshima during the Korean war. She had made many friends among the faculty and students.

As one of their special community projects, our students presented this same program to hundreds of elementary school children at the American Culture Center (still left over from the

American Occupation). The YWCA girls had worked very hard to paint a lovely mural which covered one side of the auditorium, and another group made the figures for a manger scene placed in one corner.

We invited the members of our after-school Bible classes to special parties at our mission house. I helped some of the Christian students to present special programs with slides at a hospital and musical recordings at a school for the blind.

My first Christmas in a foreign land was made very special when I was awakened by hearing familiar Christmas carols sung by lovely young voices under my window. When I looked out, I saw colorful Japanese lanterns with lighted candles which shone on the faces of young people from my church. Their custom was to meet at the church on Christmas Eve for a celebration. Then after a few hours of sleep--on the floor--they started out before dawn to sing carols at the homes of church members. The main celebration of Christmas took place in churches rather than homes, since December 25th was a regular workday. I was also moved by what the young woman helper of our next door missionary did on Christmas day. There were some men and women workers doing the heavy digging and lifting to make the wall around our new school building. Myoko San, who had become a Christian after coming to work at our school, called in these workers and served them hot chocolate as a way of letting them have a part in her Christmas day. She explained to them that Christmas is a time of showing kindness and giving gifts, and she wanted to share something with them.

In spite of all the positive influences of Christianity in our school, the administration and the Christian teachers struggled with the problem of how to provide an excellent academic curriculum and at the same time how to help the students to have a real understanding of the Christian faith. At first I wondered why so many non-Christian parents chose to send their daughters to this Christian school. I found that many Japanese people had no strong religious convictions, even though they would tell you their family was Buddhist. It was primarily a secular society with a strong belief in science and education. After the long years of deprivation during the war, most people had as their goal to become prosperous. Japanese people thought of Christians as good people who might be able to teach their children good moral principles. Of course there were some parents who objected if their daughters became interested in being baptized and joining a church. They thought it might be a hindrance to making a good marriage. But there were some parents who seemed to be glad if their daughters found a faith that gave meaning to their lives.

Some of our non-Christian teachers engaged in serious arguments about Christianity. But I began to realize that those who seemed to be the most anti-Christian were those who were struggling in their own mind about whether to believe in it or not. Those who were indifferent didn't bother to argue. The most surprising event during my first three years was when our head teacher announced that he was becoming a Christian. All of us admired him as a true leader and as a very intelligent man. But when I first went there, he was the one who argued the most and asked the most questions about the Bible and the Christian beliefs. He and his family became strong members of one of the churches in the community.

No one became a Christian suddenly in that secular society. I knew of some girls who had been through our junior high and high school and college who decided to be baptized just before they graduated. They often said they had complained of having to attend daily chapel, but when they looked back on their school days, they felt that was what they would miss the most. Some girls became Christians years later after they had children of their own. They said they wanted their children to know the kind of atmosphere they had experienced in our Christian school.

By the time I went to Japan, the church was autonomous and not dependent on mission boards except for some emergency aid in the post-war years when so many of the churches and schools had to be rebuilt. Missionaries were only sent at the invitation of the church in Japan. The exceptions were some of the sect groups who saw an opportunity to start a new church in the post-war years when there was such an interest in Christianity. The established denominations which had been in Japan for 100 years were still asking for missionaries especially to teach in church-related schools and to do pioneer evangelism where there were no churches. As I explained before, during the 60's and 70's the churches and Christian schools in Japan set up a fund to help subsidize the work of missionaries. At present Japanese Christians are paying the salaries and the housing for short-term teachers who come from America after they are screened by the mission boards. The only expense for the American church is their travel expense. So it seems that Japan has come full circle from the Tokunaga era when all foreigners were banned and Christianity was a forbidden religion.

15. Important Festivals In Japan

Christmas has always been a magical time for me. There was the fun of bringing out the traditional Christmas tree ornaments, and seeing the glow of the lights on the tree, the joy of singing carols on Christmas Eve, and hearing again the well-loved stories of the Nativity. My first Christmas in Japan was full of celebrations at school and at church. We did all we could to make it a meaningful time for our students. They dramatized the nativity story in our chapel service, and they had lots of parties in their various groups. Since Christmas day is not a holiday in Japan, church people celebrate on the Sunday before Christmas by sharing a festive meal together after the service.

But as New Year's approached, I realized this was the most important holiday in Japan. When I went downtown during the days just before New Years, there was a feeling of expectation and a flurry of activity that permeated the atmosphere. Everyone hoped to go home if possible, in the same way that we do at Christmas time. New Year's is not just one day, but most people have at least three days off. Even if they go back to work on the fourth day, they don't do much except go the rounds and give greetings to each one in the company, have a drink together and then go home. On the second day there is a procession of trucks loaded with the first products of the new year all decorated with colorful banners, slowly making their way down the main streets.

During the last part of December, the companies have end of the year parties, a time for forgetting what is past before starting the new year. They say this is one time when workers can speak frankly to their bosses and get away with it. This happens after all of them have done a good deal of drinking. They are usually careful to have a designated driver or else to go home by taxi.

Because it is important to start the new year with a clean slate, people try to pay all their bills by the end of the year and clean their house from top to bottom. During the last week the streets are crowded with busy shoppers. People buy gifts and housewives shop for food to prepare for the many guests expected, as well as to be sure to have enough staples on hand. Except for hotels, everything is closed for those two or three days. I was glad to see that even the mom and pop stores that seem to be open seven days a week close down to give the owners a few days of needed rest. Doctors and nurses manage to have some free time, as every patient who can possibly be moved is sent home for a few days.

I often saw housewives outdoors scrubbing the doorposts, washing windows, and even washing the clapboards on the front of the house. Even though I didn't feel it necessary to do any big house cleaning, as I had worked hard to get ready for Christmas, I sometimes couldn't help getting into the mood of those around me. So I might spend some time going through my dresser drawers or cleaning out my desk during those last days when I had no meetings.

Housewives are busy up to the last minute preparing New Year's food which they stash away in layered lacquer boxes ready to serve. Except for the soup, most of the food is served cold as it is all prepared ahead of time. There are hard boiled eggs cut in fancy shapes, mounds of sweet potatoes topped with cooked chestnuts, various kinds of "osushi" served on trays, large shallow plates of vegetables flavored with soy sauce and sugar, bits of cooked fish and chicken, and an expensive kind of fish eggs--a kind of caviar. I was invited to a home where I could watch the interesting process of making "omochi", the one food which is considered a must for the New Year's breakfast. They cooked glutinous rice in a large pot until it was a gooey mass. Then they transferred it to a hollowed out wooden stump mounted on a sturdy base so the pounding could be done with abandon. One of the men took a long-handled wooden mallet and began to pound, as one of the women skillfully turned it with moistened hands. They chanted in rhythm to keep in perfect harmony so the man never hit her fingers. When it was the right consistency, they rolled it out on a counter dusted with rice flour. Then the children got into the act by pulling off bits of the rice to fashion it into round balls. It reminded me of American children helping their mother with making Christmas cookies. These rice balls were placed in shallow wooden boxes to be stored for use during the coming holidays. As there is no flavor to the rice balls, they place them over a grill or in the oven and heat them until they puff up and become crisp. Then they dip them in hot water and roll them in barley flour and sugar, or just dip them in soy sauce and sugar. At breakfast they drop the puffed up balls into the boiling "miso" soup. Children often brag to each other on new Year's day to see who managed to eat the most "omochi" that morning. People get rather substantial bonuses which become part of their salary. Often they are large enough to enable families to buy a big household item. Companies give year-end gifts to customers, and individuals give gifts to anyone to whom they feel obligated. On New Year's day each child receives a lucky gift envelope with money from parents, grandparents, and other relatives. So they have fun planning how to spend it. Some parents teach children to save at least a part of it, thus contributing to the culture of saving which has been a feature of Japanese life.

On New Year's morning each family member bows to the elders and they recite the proper greetings to say thank you for everything received in the year that is past and to ask them for favors in the coming year. There is much bowing and reciting the greetings to everyone whom a person meets for the first time that year--even on the street. This continues through the early part of the year. On New Year's eve there is a fire festival on the nearby island of Miyajima. The first year I was there, Miss Hirose took some of us to see that glorious spectacle. Everyone on the island had prepared cone-shaped torches made of thin wood and filled with pine branches and kindling wood doused with kerosene. Hotels and stores had huge torches carried by six to ten men on their shoulders. Ordinary families had a small one which the father and his little boy could carry. When the Shinto priest came down from the shrine on the mountain top where the sacred fire never went out, people rushed to be the first to light their torches from the hot coals he carried. Then they jogged along the shore of the Inland Sea rhythmically chanting as they went. I remember how cold it was and how good the warmth of those fires felt as we dangled our legs from a high place where we had climbed to get a good view. I loved seeing small boys feeling very important as they helped their fathers carry a torch. Everyone seemed to be thoroughly enjoying this parade of lighted torches. Tradition has it that this will prevent homes and stores from having any fires during the coming year. I thought that was based on good psychology, as they had a chance to play with fire and get it out of their system. Finally they doused the torches in buckets of water and took the burned-out torch to be set up in front of their home or place of business.

In later years I often took American visitors to this festival, and sometimes we stayed in one of the Japanese inns on the island. Streetcars and ferries ran all night because it was a tradition to climb the sacred mountain on the island to watch the sunrise. The small shops closed in the early evening, and opened at about midnight to be ready for the rush of visitors. When we looked out of our hotel window on New Year's morning, we saw a never-ending stream of women clad in colorful kimonos as families came to pray at the Shinto shrine for good fortune in the new year. Almost everyone who could afford a kimono, wore it on New Year's day and sometimes on the second and third day. Even some of the men wore traditional dark kimonos and "geta" (Japanese footwear). The hotel served us the New Year breakfast which included "miso" soup with "omochi" floating in it.

On my first New Year's day Miss Hirose invited the missionaries for a traditional New Year's breakfast at her home. She was a real career woman with no time for cooking, but her widowed sister kept house for her and cooked very tasty meals when she entertained. In later years when I lived alone, I often joined with the dormitory matron and her assistant who were unmarried women, as I wanted to be a part of the festive feeling instead of eating breakfast alone.

My Japanese teacher, Mrs. Harano, invited some of the new missionaries to their very small house for dinner during the holidays. Her husband was a minister who had contracted TB during the war. As I related earlier, I had been introduced to his family by a Canadian pastor who was his classmate at McGill

Seminary in Montreal. They lived in one of the Schmoe houses which had been built in the early post-war years. Floyd Schmoe was a Quaker who had a concern to reach out to the people who had suffered so much in Hiroshima. When he heard that the greatest need was for housing, he organized a work camp of young people to build a cluster of small wood houses which they turned over to the city to be rented to the most needy. Most of them went to war widows, but the Harano's who had four children, qualified because of his ill health. It became a custom for this family to invite me every year during the New Year holidays. I always marveled that she could produce a tasty New Year's feast on their limited income and that they could manage to make room for three or four of us in their cramped quarters. When I returned for a visit in 1986, it was a joy to see Mrs. Harano, now a widow, living in a comfortable new house with her son and his family as he is now a professor of French at the city university.

Another family who usually invited me at New Year's was a rather young widow, Mrs. Kanda, whose three daughters attended our school. She had helped out at the mission house while she attended our college in pre-war years. Her husband died of TB while the girls were still quite young. She was able to make a living by teaching in elementary school. I always had fun playing the special New Year card game at their home. One person called out the beginning line of well-known poetry. The others seated on the floor with all the cards spread out in front of them would grab the correct card as soon as they recognized the poem. Naturally, I could not compete with the girls, as you had to be familiar with the pictures and the poems. I remember they always offered me a hot bath before our meal. This is a courtesy to guests especially at New Year's when people feel at leisure.

We missionaries laughed about an incident that happened to our one African American J-3 who came to teach music in the 1950's. One of the college teachers invited her to her home for dinner. Since it was in an outlying town, she had to take a short train trip. So the hostess wanted to offer her a bath before they ate dinner. Since her English was very limited and Charlotte, who had been there only a short time, knew very little Japanese, communication was difficult. Finally the hostess blurted out, "Are you clean?" Charlotte's startled answer was, "Yes, I'm clean. I took a bath before I came." We assured her later that no offense was meant as the hostess was offering a common courtesy.

Since it is the custom to offer prayer at a shrine or a temple at New Year's time, the Christians usually have special prayer meetings during the first week of the new year. I wrote home about my first year when our church people invited me to a home in the neighborhood.

"I went to the home of the Murakamis, one of the lovely couples who can talk to me in English at our church. Their home was one of the simple wooden houses constructed right after the war on an old army parade ground. We all sat on the floor in their tiny living room around a "hibachi" over which we could warm our hands. I marveled how everyone sat on their knees through the speeches and prayers without getting fidgety. I hadn't mastered the art yet, and I had to keep shifting from side to side. Of course I was glad when refreshments were served, as I didn't understand much of the talking. They served little plates of cookies and wrapped taffy-like candy and bowls of mandarin oranges which grow on the many islands around here. Mr. Murakami passed around his father's album which was very interesting. As a doctor who was head of a hospital, he had preserved pictures of his trip around the world when he had been sent to observe hospitals in other countries. I was impressed by the autograph from Jane Addams who had been one of my ideals during my college days. He had a newspaper clipping showing a sign, 'No more Japanese wanted here' that came from California."

In later years that church had an early morning prayer meeting at the church on New Year's morning. I remember going across town before it was light. Some of the barbershops and beauty parlors were just closing up. They stay open all night on new

Year's Eve as people want to be made beautiful after their preparations are finished. I noticed lots of people in taxis going here and there. When I left the service at about 8:30, the streets were deserted, and everything seemed strangely silent. After their hectic preparations, people like to sleep late on New Year's morning. The exceptions are those who climb a mountain to view the sunrise!

Most of the houses and hotels have festive New Year decorations. Each front door is decorated with a festoon made of pine, ferns and red berries, held together with rope and topped with a special kind of orange which symbolizes long life. Inside the house is a large round 'omochi' topped with an orange. The hotels and department stores have a tall decoration set up on both sides of the front door. It is made of bamboo poles cut in different lengths--they remind me of organ pipes--with clusters of red berries, pine branches, flowering plum branches, and a pretty purple cabbage-like flower arranged at the base. However, in recent years they have become more aware of conserving the pine trees. So the city furnishes a picture of this decoration to paste on the doorpost instead of using the real thing. Some of the larger hotels still have those decorations by the front door.

In later years I often visited some of my former students who were married and had homes of their own. It was a time when I felt free to call and ask when it would be convenient to visit them. Because there is a feeling of leisure and most housewives had prepared food for guests, it was a good time to call on them. I remember one visit which turned out to be an overnight stay. When I arrived, the young woman, Yoshiko, told me how glad she was that I could come. Her sister and their children had planned to come, but the children were sick with chicken pox and had to stay home. She felt let down not to have guests after she had looked forward to it. She had a small child still in her high chair. She invited me to stay for dinner and then she suggested I stay overnight. I protested at first, but she convinced me that there would be nothing going on that I needed to be home for. The beautiful futon laid out in the guest room looked so inviting that I agreed to stay. It is the custom to provide nightclothes for guests at any time, and she offered me a "yukata" (cotton kimono). She and her husband had lived for a few years in California where he had an import business. Now they had come back to make their home in Japan. They enjoyed talking to Americans and they spoke English well. An interesting sequel to that visit took place many years later here in Amherst when a college student from Japan called to ask me if I remembered a student named Yoshiko Myoda. When I told her I did, she said, "That is my mother." So it turned out that she had been that little girl in the high chair when I visited her family. She didn't know I lived here when she chose the University of Massachusetts. But she met a Japanese woman who told her there was a woman here who had taught in Hiroshima and she thought it might be the school where this girl had studied. Since she was at the university for four years, I tried to be her American grandmother.

Another important holiday when almost everyone tries to go back home is "obon," a festival of the dead, which is observed in August. At that time, when the spirits of the dead would return for a few days, everyone visits the graves to clean up around them and decorate them with paper lanterns. A lighted candle is placed in the lantern to light the way for the dead to return. A plate of food is usually placed nearby, though in modern times they use artificial food made of plastic.

During my first summer one of the girls who had shared the work camp with me, invited me to her home to celebrate this important festival in August. She took me to see the lantern parade along the river when people float hundreds of paper lanterns mounted on plywood with a lighted candle inside. Relatives pay a small fee to have the name of their dead loved ones written on the lantern and thus send the spirits forth after spending a few days with the family. We rented a rowboat which gave us a wonderful view unhampered by the crowds which absolutely filled the streets. A Shinto priest in a brocaded garment with the black helmet-like traditional headdress stood in dignified silence as he beat on the drum in his boat going up and down the river. It made an eerie sound. This was meant to notify the gods that the spirits were returning.

It was a strange mixture of gaiety and solemnity. The procession to the graves and the priest leading the lantern parade contrasted with the festive air on the streets afterward. When we got out of our boat, families were walking up and down the river banks where booths to sell food and souvenirs had been set up. Children dressed in their colorful summer kimonos were eating such dainties as dried fish toasted over a charcoal fire, bits of meat on sticks cooked in a large stewing pot or pink and white cotton candy. There were booths containing toys and souvenirs for children, as well as the favorite summer treat, dishes of crushed ice covered with a sweet syrup colored red, yellow and green. The ice-crushing machine reminded me of an old-fashioned coffee grinder.

Spectacular fireworks were set off over the river. My student guided me to her home for the evening meal where I met her family for the first time. Then we walked to the village square where they had erected a decorative shrine lighted by Japanese paper lanterns. All the families were walking about on the streets. My student explained that the dancing wouldn't really get under way until midnight. So she suggested we go back to her house to sleep for awhile and then come back to see the dancing which might last all night.

At her house I had my first experience with a mosquito net which most people used in summer. We had to hang up a large green net which stretched from each of the corners of the bedroom creating a sort of musty bower where we lay on our futons on the floor. This made the summer night even more unbearably hot. Her father woke us up before midnight and when we went back to the village square, the scene had changed. Two huge drums hung in a framework with two men in kimonos beating them using a rhythmic dance step in between the powerful blows. They had thin towels tied round their heads which is a symbol indicating that they are really in earnest about the task at hand. Some women were singing the special song, accompanying themselves on the "samisen," a three stringed banjo-like instrument which sounded rather weird to my Western ears. A few women and girls were beginning the slow rhythmic dance, making a huge circle all around the drums. The dance looked very simple, but when I tried it, I discovered how difficult it was to coordinate hands and feet. It did give me real satisfaction when some years later, I managed to master this dance with the help of a persistent elderly Japanese man who wouldn't let me give up.

That night we stayed only a short time as we both felt too sleepy to wait to see how long it might continue. So we went back and settled down again under that huge mosquito net. This was one of the good by-products of taking part in the summer work camp. Without that shared experience I would never have been invited to the student's home. It gave me another opportunity to feel a part of the Japanese community.

16. Japanese Food

Since Miss Gaines had trained the mission house cook in American cuisine, I seldom had the opportunity to eat Japanese food in my early years in Japan. There were times when we went to school conferences or outings where Japanese meals were served. At first it was hard for me to get used to vegetables and meat and fish being served cold, and especially cold rice. Since at that time, food was usually cooked over a charcoal-burning pot called a "shichirin," or over a small gas plate, I think the housewife cooked one item at a time and set it aside until the whole meal was done. So it would have been difficult to serve everything hot at once. Rice was almost always served hot, as they had a special place in the kitchen for cooking it. A large inverted metal pot was built into a place with a fire box fueled by wood under it.

In recent years they developed the electric rice cooker which keeps rice hot for a long time. But one of the favorite foods for picnics was "sushi," always called "o-sushi" using the honorific "o." Now that it's popular in America, most Americans think it means raw fish. But the basic "sushi" is rice flavored with sugar and vinegar as it is being cooled. After the rice is cooled, it may be made into four different kinds of "sushi." Rolled sushi is made by laying a sheet of crisp black dried seaweed on a piece of bamboo matting. The flavored cooled rice is spread over that. Then it is covered with bits of cooked vegetables, cooked fish and thin strips of egg omelet. This is rolled up like a jelly roll. The next step is to remove the bamboo matting and cut it into discs which are easy to eat by hand or with chopsticks. Another kind is scattered sushi where the vinegared sweet rice is served in a large shallow bowl with the vegetables, fish, egg, and bits of seaweed scattered over the top. "Inari zushi" is made by tamping the rice into small pockets of fried tofu which is a light brown color like a fox. The most expensive kind, rice ball sushi served at "sushi" bars is made by placing small bits of delicate raw fish on top of oval balls of the flavored rice with a bit of green horseradish as relish. If a person happens to swallow that horseradish all in one mouthful, it burns all the way down.

When I think of food being served cold, I remember one of our all-Japan missionary conferences which was held in a large Japanese inn. Though they served mostly Japanese food, they tried to give us a Western-style breakfast. It gave us a shock to see plates with a beautiful fried egg and toast, all set out on trays in a pantry which we passed on our way to morning worship at 7:00 A.M. Evidently it had been prepared at about 5:00 AM., though we didn't eat it until about 8:00 o'clock. The committee asked the manager if we could have hard boiled eggs the next day as they would stay warm a little longer.

At our school retreats and other gatherings, a favorite dish was "curry rice" which they always called by that English name. (It was probably imported from India). When they served the plates with big mounds of warm rice covered with the steaming stew made with beef and lots of potatoes, carrots, and onions, flavored with curry, I thought this time we could have food that was hot. But to my dismay, they had introductions, and various speeches which seemed to go on and on, while I watched that food cool off. What is called "aisatsu" (greetings) is always very important at any kind of gathering. So we had to endure a certain amount of ceremony before we could enjoy the food.

A favorite food for special occasions, especially in cold weather, is "sukiyaki" which is always served hot. It is cooked at the table in one large pan set on a charcoal heater, or nowadays on a gas plate. I still remember my first taste of that food when the students cooked it outdoors at the first fall outing I attended. We sat alongside a flowing river not far from the city. When I watched my home room group start to prepare the meal, it seemed as if they had brought everything except the kitchen sink: a cutting board, a fry pan and a large wide knife called a "hocho" which they used to cut up the many green vegetables after they had carefully washed them in the river. Into the pan they placed very thin strips of beef which they sautéed over the fire, and then they added Chinese cabbage, spinach, and green onions, along with transparent noodles and tofu, each arranged beautifully in separate compartments. Over this they poured generous amounts of soy sauce, sugar, and rice wine. When the vegetables were barely cooked, they gave us each a raw egg to break into a small dish. Then they served us some of the hot meat and vegetables which we put into the beaten egg. I have to admit that I had a mental block about eating the raw egg, though they assured me that the hot food partially cooked the egg. This also cooled the hot meat and vegetables enough to make them easier to eat. I discovered there are a lot of winter dishes cooked at the table and always served hot. These became my favorites, though after many years, I began to enjoy most of their food, and to appreciate the wide variety of their cuisine.

As younger missionaries joined our mission family, they had a different attitude from our pre-war missionaries. They were very eager to try the various kinds of Japanese food. By that time our cook was Ikeda San, the daughter of the veteran cook who had retired to live with her son. They persuaded her to make one Japanese meal a week for our dinner. She was reluctant at first, as she was afraid we wouldn't like it. But she gained confidence when she saw how much we enjoyed these meals. These young women also sought out the best restaurants which served Japanese cuisine, and I got acquainted with many different dishes.

Dottie Seest, who was there when I came, said that she missed the corner drug store or ice cream parlor she had enjoyed in her home town. As a substitute, she often dropped in on one of the many tea shops around town. Along with tea, they served nothing more exciting than the many kinds of bean cakes. As I've already indicated, I found these to be beautiful but overly sweet and rather "blah." One time I went with some students to visit a cake factory as I called it. This is the way I described it in a letter to my family:

> "They put a very sweet substance made from beans and sugar in all their fancy cakes. They make the most artistic little cakes I have ever seen, though they are too sweet for my taste. Each one represents something in nature such as roses, hydrangeas, persimmons, iris, ocean

waves or sometimes a basket. They say it takes a man about four years to become skilled in making these brightly colored cakes. You should see the kind they make for a wedding. It is a real work of art with flowers all over it, and a crane at the top, the symbol of good luck."

There were also good coffee shops, especially those which played classical records continuously. Many college students frequented these shops, as anyone who bought a cup of coffee could feel free to stay as long as he liked. Customers would request their favorite records as they sipped their coffee.

Ice cream was hard to find in those early days, except for a watery ice milk which vendors sold on station platforms. We were warned to avoid this product because of doubtful sanitation. But after a year or so, one downtown shop acquired a soft ice cream machine from Sweden. We considered this a treat to be able to buy a real ice cream cone that was safe to eat.

Amazing changes took place during the years I lived in Japan. Japanese companies began to market ice cream in many flavors, and to dress up many exotic kinds of sundaes garnished with banana slices, oranges, and other fruit, sometimes topped by a circle of pudding. Once the young son of my former colleague in Vermont visited me on his way back from a stint in the Peace Corps in Korea. Since they had not been able to get good ice cream in Korea, he and his friend enjoyed patronizing one of the ice cream parlors every evening in Hiroshima, giving them a chance to sample the creative concoctions on the menu. They said when the waitress brought out these delicious creations on the tray, they felt like applauding.

Cakes and pastries have become much more delicious and varied. In the many coffee and cake shops, an array of French pastry and all kinds of luscious cakes and cookies are displayed in glass cases. Some Japanese students have told me that when they come to America, these varied confections in the coffee shops are one of the things they miss most.

By the time I arrived in Japan, bread had already become popular as the government advocated eating wheat at one meal instead of rice. One Japanese bakery in town had sent some of their bakers to Denmark to learn how to make good bakery products. One or two skilled Danish bakers came to this bakery to provide atmosphere and teach their methods to the Japanese workers. As all Japanese people were familiar with Hans Christian Andersen's fairy tales, they named their bakery "Andersen's." We enjoyed shopping there for their tasty breads and pastries. In some cities there were also German bakeries. So Japanese bakers tended to make their bread more like Europeans. It had real substance unlike our air-filled Wonder bread.

In my early days in Japan various kinds of food were extremely scarce. Crackers, cheese, canned tomatoes, and other canned foods were rarely available. We looked forward to our trips to Tokyo or to Kobe where they had overseas stores which carried such items, although they were fairly expensive. Frozen food had not appeared on the market yet, but we could always get fresh fruits when they were in season. One Japanese friend who had lived in America told me he thought they valued fresh fruits and vegetables more because they could be bought only in season. We looked forward to the mandarin oranges which became ripe in the fall and winter as well as the giant strawberries and luscious peaches in early summer. Some kind of fruit was always available including figs, persimmons and 20th century pears which were new to me. These delicious pears were said to be a cross between a pear and an apple. They were round in shape like apples but they tasted like juicy pears except the flesh was more crisp. At first bananas were so expensive that they were used only as gifts. But later they were imported from both Taiwan and North America and they became much more reasonable.

Once at the teachers' fall outing, we went to a nearby farm to gather mushrooms which grow under pine trees in certain places. They charged a fee to enter. Then everyone tried to gather some of the large mushrooms which were very hard to spot. Included in the fee was a supper of mushrooms cooked in "sukiyaki." But most people also found some to take home. When they told the farmer I had not found any, he took pity on this "gaijin" (foreigner) and showed me where I could find some.   I had looked at the same place without seeing any.

One time I joined the staff of the Christian social center on an outing to gather chestnuts at a farm in the area. In the same way, after we had gathered some for ourselves, the people at the farm prepared a tasty supper of rice cooked with chestnuts and chicken, flavored with soy sauce.

In November my Bible class went on an outing to one of the nearby islands where the juicy "mikan" (mandarin oranges) grew in abundance.   We took the ingredients for making "sukiyaki" as well as the charcoal burner on which to cook it. In return for the fee which we paid to enter the orchard, we could pick as many oranges as we could eat. But if we picked more than we could eat there, we were obliged to have them weighed so we could pay for them. I found that just as people were pleased when I made an effort to speak their language, they were also happy when I learned to appreciate their food. It seemed to bring me closer to the people around me.

17. No More Hiroshimas

Americans were received very cordially in the early postwar years, but that feeling suddenly changed in 1960 just before the US-Japan Security Treaty was to be renewed. Student riots broke out all over the country, and we became aware of strong anti-American feelings.

There had always been strong anti-war feeling throughout the country after the war. On the skeleton of the ruins of the industrial museum, which marked the epicenter of the bombing, were the bold letters of their post war motto, "NO MORE HIROSHIMAS" written in English. This was at the entrance to the peace park which had been placed in the center of the downtown area, as part of Mayor Hamai's 25-year plan to rebuild the city.

At the center of the park was the Peace Museum and behind the museum there was a wide path leading to the replica of an ancient tomb. Inside were written the names of all those whose bodies could never be recovered. On a plaque are words which can be translated:

> "May you rest in peace. We will never commit this sin again."

When asked about whom the "we" refers to, they said, "We hope it includes the whole world." There are always flowers and incense at this site. Japanese people feel it is very important to pray at the graves of their ancestors. But they have no graves for those family members whose bodies evaporated at the time of the bomb. When world leaders come to the city, they usually lay a wreath in front of this monument. Just beyond the monument is a reflecting pool and an eternal flame which burns continuously. Throughout the grounds, there are many statues depicting scenes of that fateful day. One is a mother shielding her small child and a baby in arms as she flees the burning city.

Inside the museum the exhibit begins with a brief history of the development of the atom bomb. At the center is a miniature model of the city as it looked just after the bombing. It resembles a desert with only the stark skeletons of the few reinforced concrete buildings which were left standing. In glass cases one can see models dressed in he actual tattered remnants of kimono of some of the victims. Twisted glass bottles, a discolored bamboo tree affected by the radiation, and many other objects which had been through the intensive heat and radiation show what happened to materials. The cement step from a bank building contains the permanent shadow of a person who had been sitting there when the powerful atom rays caused him to evaporate. There are many pictures portraying the horror of the effect on human beings--people with strips of skin hanging from their outstretched hands, faces and backs; people with keloid burns, and corpses of children whose charred bodies lay spread-eagled on the road. At the end of the exhibit, there are charts and figures suggesting peaceful uses of this awesome power which science has released.

Another wing has now been added to the museum in which they show some of the events that led up to the war--Japan's invasion of China and the rape of Nanking. The purpose is to help the younger generation have a more even-handed view of the war. But there are some people who object to that in the same way that U.S. veterans objected to the Smithsonian exhibit, planned for the 50th anniversary of the bombing of Hiroshima. That exhibit was to show some of the horrors of the atom bomb along with the plane, the Enola Gay, which dropped the bomb on Hiroshima. But it ended up showing only the plane without any scenes of what happened to people.

It is easy to understand why the Japanese who survived the bombing have such a deep yearning to renounce war, and to build a peaceful society. They welcomed the new constitution which renounced war and forbade them from having an army or from sending troops outside their borders. This was practically dictated by MacArthur and those who directed the Occupation. But within a few years, when the outbreak of the Korean war brought on such strong anti-Communist fears in America, this policy was reversed. Japan was urged to re-arm. There was also what was called a "red purge" of many of the labor union leaders and others who had been favored by the Occupation because of their opposition to the militaristic policy of Japan during the war. Many of them had Marxist ideas which became anathema to the U.S. leaders. Even though Japan did agree to raise an army, they held on to Article 9, the peace clause in their constitution, insisting on calling it a Self-Defense Force.

Here are quotations from some of my students' essays in those early post-war years:

"Before the Second World War, Japan was a militaristic country. ...Statesmen made a puppet of Japanese people. ...Directly after the War, Japanese people's minds became blank by the defeat and social confusion and economic poverty. And our people still have no prop for their soul. The thing that props people's soul is faith. Our Japanese need to have faith. ...Though fifteen years passed since the defeat, I am afraid the danger of war remains and there is a little battle somewhere in the world all the time. So our generation must make places good to live in, and we have to do our best for permanent peace."

Another one wrote:

"I lost my father in World War II. ...Now I think about him very often. Was he a gentleman or a terrible man? A few weeks ago I read letters which were written by my father from the theater of war to my mother. They were hurried notes. ...But I understood that my father was strong and very, very tender. I don't know father's love and he didn't know his child. The responsibility rests upon war. I had not a fright of war, but I know misery and sadness after the war. Now there are two worlds. We are in a dangerous condition because these two worlds have very fine arms. Nowadays science is making rapid progress. But men's hearts make little progress. Because east side and west side may blow up a quarrel. ...Delegates from the two worlds cannot lose their face. They have no room in their hearts. ...So we must teach them that all the world wishes no more war on the earth. All people in the world must cry 'peace', in one voice."

No country welcomes an occupying force, but many Japanese said the leaders of the American Occupation sincerely tried to help them rebuild their country. Miss Hirose, who was recognized as an outstanding educator in Japan, told me that the Japanese educators appreciated the <u>high</u> caliber of the consultants who came during the Occupation to help them revamp their schools. From a curriculum which had taught students to believe their highest goal was to die for the Emperor, they hoped to create a curriculum which would help young people become responsible citizens in a democracy where everyone would have an equal chance to fulfill his or her potential.

With this background in mind, it is easier to understand the riots which broke out all over Japan when the time came to renew the Security Treaty. Most Americans were not very much aware of this treaty, but for Japanese it meant the fearful prospect of being drawn into war if the two great powers should begin fighting. Japan and America were pledged to defend each other in the event of war. Americans thought the Japanese should be grateful to have our powerful armies there ready to assist them, but the Japanese felt having large numbers of American military forces on bases in Japan, might be more likely to bring on an attack rather than prevent one. They believed that an unarmed Japan would be less likely to be attacked.

President Eisenhower had announced a visit to Japan just before the treaty was to be signed. Shortly before he was to go, his Secretary of State, Mr. Hagerty, came to Japan to make preparations for the visit. To the dismay of the Japanese government, he was roughed up by a rather violent protest of students at the airport carrying placards with anti-American slogans. This news hit the front pages of American newspapers. Many Americans couldn't understand why Japan should turn against her benefactor who had helped them recover from the destruction of the war. The Japanese government was embarrassed that the police had not been able to prevent the outbreak. They expressed their regret, but they asked President Eisenhower to postpone his visit, as they couldn't guarantee his safety.

When I wrote one of my general letters to church people in July 1960, I tried to explain that the causes of the protests were more complicated than simple anti-American feelings. I told them that my Japanese friends urged me to inform them that the riots were not mainly anti-American, but rather anti-war. I reported also that U.S. reporters who walked among the crowds found that even those carrying anti-American placards were friendly and quite willing to talk to Americans. When I discussed this with my students, they assured me that they liked Americans but they didn't like the American policy. At that time there was a national student union in the universities which was admittedly leftist in its sentiments. Only a small percentage of students were active in that group, but because they were so well organized, they led the protests. Other students joined in because they wanted to speak out for peace. During that time of tension, some of our Christian Japanese teachers asked the missionaries to meet with them so they could explain their point of view to us. This is the letter I wrote to American churches at that time:

> "My Japanese colleagues said as everyone does that the first and most deep-seated cause of their opposition to the Security Treaty is their terrible fear of nuclear war. They feel that modern war is in a whole different category from any wars that we have known, and that war would be the ultimate evil. Having American troops on Japanese soil makes it seem more likely that Japan could be dragged into a war, if the two great powers should ever come to actual warfare. They have an almost naive belief that if they stay unarmed and remain neutral, they will be allowed to go their own way in peace. In fact, they cling to the idea given them by General MacArthur during the Occupation that they might be able to lead the way by being an example to the rest of the world. They say they realize the risk that disarmament involves, but they prefer that risk to the way of war.

"Of course the other big cause for the demonstrations was the widespread distrust of the Kishi government, especially after they rammed through the vote in a most undemocratic way. It is hard to say which was worse-- the Socialists who used force to keep the speaker from convening the Diet, or the ruling Liberal Democratic party which used its power to call in the police and then took a vote when all the opposition had been forcibly ousted. Some people say if Kishi had handled the whole thing more skillfully, the general public would have accepted the treaty, though reluctantly, without any uprising.

"I am sure that most Japanese people were truly ashamed of what happened to Hagerty. They are particularly proud of Japanese hospitality which goes to any lengths to make a visitor feel welcome. Everyone would have gladly welcomed Eisenhower and would have felt honored by his visit if only it had not been timed to coincide with the vote on the treaty. The student population of Japan is made up of the war babies who started to school when things were in a state of upheaval. Having been ordered by the Occupation to turn everything upside down, the teachers trained in the old ways were at a loss as to how to proceed in the new atmosphere of freedom. Miss Hirose has commented in a recent article that this generation learned freedom without learning the responsibility that goes with it. And when one sees the fist-fighting that often goes on in the Diet itself, it is not surprising that these students also resort to force when they feel frustrated at not being able to make their voices heard.

"Our teacher friends explained that it has always been considered bad taste to talk too much about politics. Thus the general public has a great ignorance of political matters even though they have a surface knowledge of events. Although the Meiji Revolution brought freedom of a sort to Japan more than 100 years ago, it was a revolution from the top down, and the general public didn't hammer it out themselves as our American forebears did. Then again after the war, the Occupation gave them a democratic constitution but they still don't have the 'feel' of democracy. When the government does something they don't like, they still feel helpless to reach the people 'higher up'. They lack the patience to depend on the slow, cumbersome democratic methods of securing change.

"Many of the Christians have joined in these demonstrations, or they have put on their own peaceful demonstrations because they feel they must witness for peace and stand up and be counted. The young Christians in their 30's are ashamed when they think of how the church blindly followed the militarist government in the last war. They believe the church must become more politically educated and speak out on issues such as this.

"I've been telling you about one segment of the people. Of course there are many people who, though they want to hold on to the peace clause in the constitution, maintain that it would be folly to cut off their treaty with the U.S. now. The president of our large government university here is in favor of the treaty. He accused many of the college professors of following the students and he urged them to pour water instead of oil on the fire. Miss Hirose believes that some kind of military security is necessary at this time, though she hopes that a general disarmament can be gradually brought about. On the whole, the business people favor the treaty and they have been quite worried about the slump in trade that followed the riots. They know the life-blood of Japan is trade with other countries and that this in turn depends on a stable government.

"One can't live in Hiroshima and not feel great sympathy with people who can't bear to face a nuclear war. Also I can't help sympathizing with their hopeless feeling when they realize that what little gains they've made in achieving a better standard of living would be wiped out if they are forced to pour money into preparation for a present-day war. But at the same time, I can't help feeling that they do not have a realistic picture of the political scene as it is, and that they do not understand how international Communism works. Though they keep reminding us there are only a handful of Communists in Japan, I can't help remembering how much a handful can do when they are dedicated people with a single-minded purpose and are working in fertile soil where the people are dissatisfied with their government. The more we see of the problems in this new democracy, the more we realize how hard it is to have the fruit of democracy without the roots. True democracy must be rooted in a concern for one's neighbor and respect for each individual as a child of God. Where these roots are not present, it is too likely to be a surface democracy having the form but not the basic substance that is needed."

As expressed in this letter I had mixed feelings as I tried to defend the policy of my own country. At the same time I could understand the feelings of the Japanese people who were so hopeful of building a peaceful world. I continued to feel this ambivalence when the Vietnam War broke out causing even more violent student protests.

During that time the radical element of the student union was able to barricade many universities causing a virtual shutdown of classes. Because of the strong tradition of not calling in the police to interfere in university matters, the administration seemed almost helpless to deal with that crisis. Most of the Christians strongly opposed the bombing of village people in that beleaguered country of Vietnam which had suffered from more than 20 years of warfare. The fact that U.S. planes took off from Okinawa made the Japanese very fearful of being drawn into it.

A group of Christian pastors wished so strongly to talk face to face with American Christians about their mistaken policy, that they raised money among the small struggling churches to send a delegation to talk to their counterparts in American churches. One of the missionaries went along as an interpreter. He tried to set up meetings and small group dialogues, but unfortunately they went during the summer months when most churches were on vacation. The Japanese wanted to confess to the Americans how they had mistakenly followed their government into World War II without protest. They sincerely wanted to warn the American Christians not to do the same thing. They tried to help them see how it looked from the point of view of Southeast Asians when America used its great power to destroy village people who were trying to carry on their farms and businesses. They told them it was a civil war that could not be solved by a third party. They realized the bombing would not stop Communism but would rather have a tendency to throw them into the arms of the Communists. When I spoke about this to American church people during my furlough, I found they had never heard of it. Some of them said they wished they had known about it.

Eventually the student union lost its power, and order was restored in the colleges. There was a spin-off from the radical group which infected the Kyodan churches. Because the leaders of the church agreed to have a Christian pavilion at the 1970 Osaka Expo, some of the younger pastors accused them of cooperating with those who placed material prosperity before principle. They argued that the prosperity being celebrated in the Expo had come about because of Japan trade to help support the American army in the Korean war. They thought the Christians should boycott the whole event rather than taking part in it. Others said it was an opportunity to witness to the work of the church in Japan. This caused violent outbreaks at the annual meeting of the Tokyo and Osaka districts which took over 20 years to heal. They were not able to have the annual meetings of the Tokyo and Osaka districts because of disruption by seminary students, young pastors and laymen. The protesters believed it was their conscientious duty to speak out against what they called the worship of Baal, as they called the forces which had brought economic gain to Japan through trade based on war. In spite of the long struggle which threatened to divide the church, the local churches carried on their regular worship and other activities.

From experiencing these explosive events, I learned that whenever anything happens in the United States, it has repercussions all over the world. I also found that at least in the industrialized nations people know a lot more about America than we know about their countries. I learned also it is superficial to judge each nation by categorizing them as pro-American or anti-American. It is important to know the causes of their actions which seem to be anti-American to us. When I returned to America, I tried to echo the voices of the survivors of Hiroshima and Nagasaki by doing what I could to make a world where there will be no more Hiroshimas. I wish all Americans could read the poem by Hermann Hagedorn which he published in a small book following World War II entitled, "The Bomb that Fell on America." His thesis was that the bomb which fell on Hiroshima fell also on America[6]. The final words of the poem express his belief as to the only way to save our world from nuclear holocaust:

"There is power in the human soul
When you break through and set it free.
Like the power of the atom,
More powerful than the atom.
It can control the atom.
The only thing in the world that can."

---

[6] Blanford Press, London 1947 (Out of print)

18. Hiroshima Maidens

As I gradually became more aware of all the human suffering brought about by the atom bomb which fell on this city, I was very thankful when an opportunity came for me to have a small part in helping one group of victims. This came about because of a project initiated by the pastor of Nagarekawa Church located near our school.

Soon after arriving in Hiroshima, I met this pastor, Rev. Kiyoshi Tanimoto, whose church had a historical connection with our school. In the early years the students were expected to attend services there on Sunday. Mr. Tanimoto was an interesting mixture of a person with strong evangelistic zeal and also strong social action concerns. He was one of the few pastors in the city who could speak English fairly well. He had received his theological education in America before the war. He had become famous through John Hersey's book "Hiroshima," as he was one of the five survivors interviewed for his account of the bombing. As soon as new missionaries arrived, he besieged us with opportunities to teach English in the night school that he directed in his church.

He had sponsored many other projects in the city such as a small orphanage for children whose parents had died in the bombing. He also initiated a "moral adoption" program whereby American families could provide support to children who needed help, as well as giving them encouragement by carrying on correspondence with them.

His other important project was the small Bible class he had started with a group whom he called "Hiroshima Maidens." At the time of the bomb, many teen-age school girls were at work in a section of the city very near the epicenter of the bomb. As a result, they had received massive burns that disfigured their faces and hands, and often their whole bodies. After he knew their families wanted to keep them hidden, he persuaded some of them to come to his church once a week where they could meet others with similar problems. Of course, his goal was partly to help them find a faith to live by, but he also set out to help them get needed plastic surgery. One girl had such serious injury to her eyes that she couldn't close her eyelids. He was able to get Japanese donors to provide travel to Tokyo where that girl and several others received some basic cosmetic surgery. But he was sure that if they could get to America, their looks could be substantially improved by doctors who were further along in this kind of surgery.

Because of his fame from Hersey's book, he was often visited by well-known people from America. He always made it a point to introduce them to this little group of Hiroshima Maidens. Naturally he told them about his dream to have them receive treatment in an American hospital. One of his friends was Norman Cousins, editor of the "Saturday Review of Literature," who was a strong peace activist. He made frequent trips to Japan and he was the one who had helped Mr. Tanimoto carry out the moral adoption program. When he saw these young women, he felt a strong desire to do whatever he could to help them get the best plastic surgery available.

As soon as Cousins returned to America, he set out to enlist the help of people who could make this dream come true. He found doctors at Mt. Sinai Hospital in New York who wanted to help by providing their skill and hospital beds. The next step was to find homes where the young women could stay in between treatments, as this would have to be done over a long period of time. When he appealed to the Quakers, they alerted the members of the various Friends' Meetings in the New York and Connecticut area. They soon found families who were glad to provide hospitality in between their hospital stays. The last difficult piece of the plan was to find air transportation. Finally he persuaded the Air Force to let them use one of their empty planes on its return trip from the nearby U.S. air base at Iwa Kuni. Even though it was built more for freight than for passengers, he was sure the girls would be willing to endure some discomfort in order to get to America.

When all the pieces of the puzzle came together, Mr. Tanimoto began to work out the details. First the doctors would come to

Hiroshima to give physical exams to see which of the young women had the stamina to go through this ordeal. Then he had to find a Japanese woman to be their interpreter and surrogate mother while they were in America. Mr. Tanimoto planned to accompany them, but much of his time would be used in raising more funds to take care of expenses. Fortunately they found a Nisei social worker at the ABCC (Atomic Bomb Casualty Center) who was able to go with them. She was bilingual and she had a real concern to help these young women when they found themselves in a new and difficult situation far from their families.

When the twenty five girls had actually been chosen, and their transportation was assured, there were only two weeks left to help them with language and orientation to life in America. Mr. Tanimoto appealed to one of our veteran missionaries, Mary Finch, who was fluent in Japanese, to take charge of this. When she asked me to help her, I was very glad to have even a small part in doing something to help these young women whose lives had been so changed by the bomb.

I will never forget what one of those girls said to me when I first met her:

> "I don't hate America. I just hate war. When war breaks out, terrible things happen on both sides. If our country had discovered the atom bomb first, we would probably have dropped it on your country. That is why I am determined to work for a peaceful world. We all need to work together to bring peace to the world."

In our brief contact with these young women, we soon discovered there were great differences in their personalities and in the way they reacted to their suffering. One bright-eyed petite girl had such disfigurement that she had almost no chin. Yet she was very outgoing, and she seemed to enjoy meeting people. She readily put out her misshapen little hand for a handshake, and she seemed to meet the world unafraid. In contrast, another girl always wore a face mask--the kind that Japanese regularly wore when they had a cold--and she seemed reluctant to speak to anyone. One girl had taken a job in a blind school where she said the children didn't have to look at her disfigured face. Others were doing dressmaking, and one was a hairdresser. It was a worthwhile experience to get acquainted with these twenty-five girls who came every night to our house for two weeks, sometimes in small groups, and a few times all together. Many of them couldn't even read the alphabet, and had never heard English spoken, as they went to school in wartime when English was taboo. We couldn't do much in two weeks except to teach them some greetings and brief them on American customs. We tried to give them experience in how to eat soup quietly instead of slurping it up noisily which is perfectly proper in Japan. Learning to handle a knife and fork, learning to butter a piece of bread, and many other things can be difficult for someone skilled in using chopsticks and always eating from dishes held in the hand close to the mouth.

A tour of our upstairs followed the meal with instructions as to how to take an American style bath in a tub, how to get into a bed, how to make it up, and how to use various other gadgets in an American home. When she saw our western style toilet, one girl remarked that if one were sick, it would be nice to be able to sit down instead of using the Japanese type almost level with the floor which requires a squatting position. Bathing in soapy water in a tub seems messy to them because of their custom of soaping up and rinsing outside the tub, and then soaking in clean water. But we explained that our bathrooms aren't made with drains to allow one to pour water on the floor as they do here. We always ended our sessions with English songs from the small "Sing It Again" booklets. They liked them so much that they all bought copies from the YMCA so they could sing together on the plane. Some of them asked for literature about Christianity which we provided in Japanese.

In true Japanese style, they went together and bought us each a lovely Japanese doll in a glass case as a farewell present. We were also invited to a tea when the mothers came. Each mother bowed low many times, uttering all the polite phrases of thanks. My polite phrases ran out after about the third bow, and I had to begin with the same ones over again. But all of them were sincerely appreciative, and we were glad of the opportunity to meet their mothers.

On May 5th, which is a holiday in Japan (Boys' Day now called Children's Day) we went over to the U.S. military airport at Iwa Kuni to see them off. I couldn't help thinking of the irony of the situation. It was an American B-29 that flew over Hiroshima on that fateful day in 1945, and left in its wake such destruction and suffering. And just ten years later, it was another American plane, a C-54, which flew some of the victims on an errand of mercy in an attempt to restore beauty and bring healing, both spiritual and physical. I'm sure there were some people who asked, "Why pick out these twenty-five? Why not spend the money on the prevention of war? etc." But I was glad there were enough people in our country who cared about these forgotten girls to make this project possible.

Since I went home on furlough that fall, I made a visit to the girls who were having treatment at Mt. Sinai during the time I was in New York. Seeing them with long tubes of skin attached from one part of the body to another, while waiting for it to take, made me realize what an ordeal this must be for them. But they found living with Quaker families an enjoyable and stimulating experience. They marveled that these people in a country which had so recently been their enemy, were willing to take them into their homes and treat them with so much loving kindness.

One of the tragic things that happened during the year, was the death of one of the girls on the operating table. Apparently her heart was not strong enough to take it, even though she had passed the physical test before leaving Japan. I was afraid this might jeopardize the whole project, but fortunately her family did not blame anyone. They took the attitude that it was a risk their daughter had been willing to take. Most of the girls did receive real physical rehabilitation, although all traces of the burns could not be removed. The bright-eyed girl with no chin had received a new chin, though the color of the skin was a shade different from the rest of her face.

Those whose fingers were frozen together had received enough correction to be able to use their hands efficiently. But most of them agreed that even more than the plastic surgery, the greatest gain for them was what the experience had done for their spiritual and social health. Their self-esteem was raised so they believed they could start a career or become good homemakers, and they felt ready to live normal lives.

Many families in Hiroshima did not want their sons to marry someone who had experienced radiation at close range, as they feared the effect on the children they would bear. However, several of these young women did get married, and they had normal children. Those who did not marry, managed to have a career. One young woman who lived across the street from me, started her own dressmaking business in her home and she did quite well. Her face was still scarred, but when she finished her make-up, she looked quite good. Another one who married and had two children, started a beauty parlor in her own home. She named her salon "Darien" because of the hospitality she had received in that Connecticut town. While she was there, she had helped out in a local beauty salon, and the people of Darien made her an honorary citizen before she left. She urged me to come to her salon promising me a discount. So I often went to her suburban home to get my permanents.

One young woman who showed unusual talent in design was helped by her host family to attend a well-known school of design in New York after her surgery was finished. They even assisted her in setting up a "Haute Couture" dressmaking shop in Tokyo when she returned. They hoped this would provide work for several of the other Hiroshima Maidens, and become a cooperative project. Evidently this did not last more than a few years because of personality clashes, and the perception that she expected her employees to work for rather low wages, in spite of her financial success. Eventually, Japan developed ready-made clothing so well that such dressmaking shops could not flourish as they had in the early years.

The petite bright-eyed girl with the new chin is still in America where she is bringing up her son. She stayed with the Norman Cousins family and became like a daughter to them. They were willing to help her get nurse's training, but because of her limited educational background, she found that was impossible. She settled on becoming a nurse's aide, and eventually she was able to support herself. At one time she lived briefly in California where she had a relationship with a Japanese man whom she hoped to marry. When she became pregnant, he abandoned her, and the Cousins family helped her through the birth of her son. He proved to be a very intelligent child, and probably by now he is helping to support her. She became an American citizen and a peace advocate. She also took an active part in a church. I heard her testify before Congress on TV when they were trying to pass legislation to freeze nuclear weapons production. She emphasized that she did not wish to lay blame on any country for what had happened to her, but she felt she had an obligation to do everything she could to keep this from happening to children anywhere in the world again.

Recently I discovered a book entitled "Hiroshima Maidens" which tells some of the life stories of these women after they returned to Japan. The writer is the son of the family in Darien who had hosted some of the girls. He was about eight years old at the time, and he had happy memories of these young women who had been part of his family. When he became a journalist, he set out to try to tell the rest of the story. He understood how careful he had to be in approaching the women. He assured them he would not allow any Japanese newspaper to interview them, and he would only write what they gave him permission to tell. They had been hounded by journalists when they first returned, causing them to become very wary of interviews with the media. They wanted to live normal lives and not be viewed as some kind of guinea pigs. Mr. Tanimoto did persuade some of them to cooperate in making a TV special at the time of the 20th anniversary of the project. But others chose not to take part.

The woman who had named her shop "Darien," welcomed him to Hiroshima. She trusted him enough to persuade some of the others to gather at a restaurant where they talked to him about being in his book. After I finished reading the book, I felt a bit sad that many of them had rather unhappy endings in their lives.

I had known that two or three of them had died fairly young from cancer or leukemia. But I had not kept track of all of them.

One interesting story was about a girl who received a proposal from an American man who fell in love with her. They could not really communicate very well, as her English remained limited, and he knew no Japanese. But he insisted on writing to her and telling her he was still waiting for her to say "yes." She was interested in her career and she had decided not to get married. She realized they had very little in common. But he was so insistent that he even visited her in Japan. With his lack of language, and his dislike of Japanese food, he found it very difficult. But he still did not give up. After a good many years, she began to think how nice it would be to live in a family as she remembered the pleasant times with her American family. So she accepted his proposal and came to America to get married. It was very rough at first as their life styles were so different, and they still had communication problems. At times they resorted to writing notes to each other as she found reading and writing easier than talking. But she never considered leaving him, and eventually they settled into a fairly comfortable relationship. This was one of the happier experiences even though it took such a long time.

Even though their lives did not all have happy endings, I am sure they valued that experience in America which helped to enrich their lives and widen their horizons. Though all the scars could not be completely erased, it helped to heal some of the inner scars left by their wartime years. I admire the people who put so much effort into this project even though they realized it affected only a small segment of the population. As the Quakers say,

"It is better to light a candle than to curse the darkness."

19. Vietnam Project

One of the spin-offs of the Hiroshima Maidens Project was the effect it had on the life of Dr. Tomin Harada, a Hiroshima surgeon who accompanied the young women to New York. He went in order to be of support to them, but also to learn more about plastic surgery. After serving in China during World War II as a military surgeon, he came back to find his hospital in Hiroshima in ruins. Seeing the great need for medical help, he managed to rebuild his hospital and start over. He found many patients who were in need of plastic surgery, but he had no special training in that branch of surgery. When he came upon an article in "Time" magazine which described a new technique used in America, he decided to experiment with it. But he still felt the need for further training.

During his stay in America, he formed friendships with some of the doctors and also with Norman Cousins. Later Cousins kept in touch with Dr. Harada to see if more help was needed for the Hiroshima Maidens. As Japan became more prosperous, he told Mr. Cousins they didn't need any more material help. But he conceived of a new project for which he hoped to enlist Cousins' cooperation. By that time he had some skill in plastic surgery. He knew that in Vietnam there must be many young people who suffered serious injuries during the long siege of war. He thought if he could help these young people, it would be a way to pay back the good will and medical help the Hiroshima girls had received from Americans. He suggested bringing one or two patients to his hospital for needed surgery. At first Mr. Cousins was enthusiastic in his support. But in the end, too much pressure was put on him by the American government which was in the midst of the Vietnam War, and he told Dr. Harada he had to refuse his request.

This was a serious disappointment for Dr. Harada, but he said it made him so angry that he just decided to go to Vietnam and see what he could do on his own. Since he couldn't speak French, and his English was limited, he had a rough time to get his message across to anyone who might work with him. He soon found that if he were willing to furnish a few Japanese motorcycles to some of the people in power, he might get some action. But he refused to stoop to bribery. Finally he ran into a Japanese journalist who took an interest in the project, and things began to happen.

In due time a young Vietnamese woman whose face had been disfigured during the French bombing, was able to come to his hospital to begin treatment for her many facial scars. A cousin who was fluent in English came along to interpret. Dr. and Mrs. Harada took them into their home. As it turned out, this young woman stayed on in Japan for several years. She became proficient enough in dressmaking to support herself. When the war finally ended, she felt it was her mission to go back to Vietnam and try to start an orphanage for the many children who would need someone to care for them. Dr. Harada's project continued for some years. The others I knew about were young high school boys. One of them had lost a leg during the war, and Dr. Harada fitted him with a serviceable artificial leg, after repairing the damage to the stump of his own leg. Many American young people living in Japan, became supporters of this work. They cooperated by having fund-raising events to help other Vietnamese to come to Japan. After one young American high school student living in Kobe, came to interview him about this work, her senior class at the Canadian Academy, an English speaking international high school in Kobe, asked him to give their commencement address.

Although he still felt his English was inadequate, he gave an inspiring talk about working for peace in one's own area. His own experience showed how one person can begin a chain reaction which might expand into a larger movement. He was strongly influenced by the peace activist, Barbara Reynolds. After her husband worked as an anthropologist at the Atom Bomb Casualty Commission ("ABCC") for a few years, they took a round-the-world trip on a yacht, which a Japanese craftsman had built for them.

His experiment was to determine whether babies who were in the womb at the time of the bomb had received any bad effects. He discovered that their heads were smaller than average, which did affect their brain power. During their voyage, they met many people who questioned them about the people of Hiroshima who had survived the bomb. They began to feel more responsible for raising the consciousness of the people of the world about the effects of atomic bombs. When they met some Quaker activists during their stay in Hawaii, they became what are known as "convinced Quakers" and joined a Friends' Meeting there.

Later, Barbara felt she was called to start a center in Hiroshima to help to minister to "hibakusha" (victims of the bomb) as well as to educate tourists from other countries about the impelling need to work toward eliminating nuclear weapons. She was able to rent a two story Japanese house which she called the World Friendship Center. Dr. Harada was impressed by Barbara's work and eventually he became chairman of the board of trustees of that center. He has helped to keep this work alive even after Barbara's death.

The center has sponsored many pilgrimages of survivors of the bomb to America and to European countries. They tried to make contact with their counterparts in Western countries through churches, schools, and fraternal organizations. Their hope was to help people understand the results of one small atomic bomb, in order to prevent the nations of the world from ever using nuclear weapons again. They have also sponsored trips to Hiroshima by American teachers and other leaders. In exchange, teachers from Hiroshima and Nagasaki have visited America, to tell of their experiences.

The Center provides a modestly priced hostel for visitors from other countries, as well as a library in English to tell the stories of many people who survived the bomb. They have been able to recruit American volunteers to take charge of the program. Usually they are retired couples or young single people who are willing to stay at least 2 years. Most of them are members of one of the historic peace churches. Of course they need the help of a Japanese interpreter to work closely with them, usually a young college graduate who has majored in English.

They sponsor lectures by peace advocates from around the world. They teach conversational English and sponsor various recreational events. They encourage visits to survivors who are in the atomic wing of the Red Cross Hospital. Although their budget has always been limited, their work has been felt in many ways around the world. As Barbara often said, it is a good example of how one pebble thrown into the water produces ripples which go on and on.

One of the other projects which Barbara sponsored was making translations of many books in Japanese written about the effects of the atom bomb on Hiroshima and Nagasaki. She recruited young people, mostly children of missionaries who had grown up in Japan and were fluent in both English and Japanese. They worked for about a year translating those books into English to form a library for research. These were deposited at Wilmington College, a Quaker college in Wilmington, Ohio. As a result, the college has established a new department in peace studies with a faculty member in charge. This provides an opportunity for research for those who wish to make their life work some kind of peace advocacy.

20. Becoming A Go-between

If anyone had told me when I went to Japan, that I would ever be a go-between to arrange a marriage, I would have laughed at them. I didn't believe in arranged marriages. I thought they happened only in unenlightened societies where women are treated as property. But after being in Japan awhile, I noticed when Japanese couples introduced themselves, they usually indicated whether their marriage was arranged or a "love marriage." To my surprise I found that statistics proved the arranged marriages are likely to be more lasting than the so-called love marriages. I saw with my own eyes that arranged marriages often become real love matches. Still I certainly never thought I would become a go-between.

However, during my second term as a missionary, in the 1960's I performed a wedding ceremony for a marriage which I had helped to arrange. It all started when I was invited to a luncheon with a group of Hiroshima Jo Gakuin graduates in Tokyo on my way back from my first furlough in America. I told them about being invited to the home of a former student in New York. I called her a modern picture bride. We all knew about the Japanese men who came here in the early 20th century years. They sent back home for pictures of young women who were willing to come to America as brides. But these young women were surprised to hear that such a thing is happening in our day.

A young man from Hiroshima had gone to New York City to take a job with one of the big Japanese department stores which started a branch there. After he had worked for five years and saved his money, he was ready to get married. But he preferred a girl from his home town. He asked his sister and her husband to find someone who could speak English well enough to get along in America. They naturally thought about a graduate of our school, who had studied under native English speakers. A good friend on our office staff suggested a recent graduate of our college who was working at the local YMCA. She had to use her English daily to communicate with their "foreign" teachers.

She agreed to correspond with this young man in New York, and they exchanged pictures. In due time, she packed up her things, flew to New York, and they were married within the week at the Japanese-American Church in Manhattan. When I visited them, they seemed to be getting along well, although she told me she had cried from homesickness in the early days of her marriage.

My former students in Tokyo were amazed. They hadn't realized that one of their contemporaries would be willing to be a "picture bride." Most of these young women were already married, but Nobuko who was almost 30 was still unmarried. After we had talked about the incident in New York, she laughingly said, "Miss Hartman, maybe you can find someone for me," although in Japanese, it was less direct than that. In any case, I had no intention of following up on her request.

Not long after that, an older missionary, Jenny Lind, who taught in Tokyo, asked me at our annual missionary conference if I knew a Christian girl who might be interested in meeting Akihiro, a young man in her Bible class. He had visited Jenny, Mary McMillan and me one weekend at a summer cottage where we were spending our vacation. We had been impressed with this clean-cut handsome young man who was intelligent and very serious minded. He was not a Christian, but he liked to study the Bible. He had asked Jenny to help him find a Christian girl. His parents in Kyoto were quite willing to arrange a marriage for him, but he didn't trust their judgment. He seemed to feel that he lived in a world quite different from theirs. Of course they were not likely to choose a Christian. Jenny really wanted to help him, but she couldn't think of a suitable candidate. Moreover, it was quite close to her retirement date when she would be leaving for America. As soon as she spoke, I thought of Nobuko. They were both living in the Tokyo area and she was a Christian girl about his age.

Jenny and I agreed that we should not try to be a real go-between, as this was a responsibility only a Japanese could fulfill. But she would be glad to invite them to dinner at her house in Tokyo. Then she would tell them they were on their own. They were surely old enough to make up their own minds.

I wrote to Nobuko and told her a little about Akihiro, and asked her if she would like to meet him. I emphasized that neither Jenny nor I would consider ourselves as their go-between. We knew one of the responsibilities was to continue as a counselor and trouble-shooter after the wedding.

When she indicated an interest in meeting him, Jenny set up the dinner in her home. When they met, something clicked, making them both eager to get better acquainted. When I met her father later at the wedding, he said his daughter had a whirlwind courtship. Once they met, they went out together almost every evening. He commented on how different it was from his own experience. He met his wife-to-be at a formal meeting, and then he met her very few times until the wedding day.

Since I lived about 12 hours from Tokyo, I hadn't heard how things were going until I received a request to meet the couple in Tokyo on my way home from my summer vacation. When I met them, they smilingly announced they were engaged. They requested me to help set up their wedding. It was then I realized that in spite of what Jenny and I had said, they really expected me to do the job of a go-between. By that time Jenny had returned to America. They were depending on me. He had written to his parents in Kyoto, as weddings in Japan are usually at the home town of the groom's parents. They had made no response. He realized they knew nothing about planning a Christian wedding, and they didn't know any ministers in Kyoto. So they chose to be silent.

Nobuko had been a member of the church where I taught an English Bible class and led a youth choir during my early years. But her parents now lived in Tokyo, and she was a member of a church near her school. Of course she didn't know any churches or pastors in Kyoto.

As I talked to them, I suddenly had a bright idea. Mr. and Mrs. Mitsui, a couple in Tokyo, had a lot of experience in being go-betweens for young couples. They had been members of the church which Nobuko and I attended in Hiroshima. Since then, he had become a judge assigned to be a research clerk for the Supreme Court in Tokyo. Whenever I came to Tokyo, they invited me to stay with them. Nobuko agreed this might be a good solution, and she would talk to them about setting up the wedding. I breathed a sigh of relief to think I would be free of that burden.

I was given one other responsibility which made me laugh. Soon after I talked with them, Akihiro wrote to ask if I would look up Nobuko's academic record at our high school and college. I was amused when he said that in thinking about choosing a wife, he had not expected his emotions to become so involved. He had pictured himself as systematically looking into her family background, her grades at school, and then deciding whether there was the proper balance required in Japanese culture for a suitable mate. It is the custom to look for a person of about the same economic, educational, and cultural background as their own family. It is important to be sure the bride had done well in school so she would be likely to produce smart children. Akihiro had fallen in love with her, and suddenly he realized he hadn't done all the proper research. When I talked to the head of the English department in our school, she assured me that Nobuko had all A grades and that Akihiro could be sure of her intelligence. When I wrote Akihiro, I told him he should be able to see for himself that Nobuko was a successful teacher and a bright young woman. But I realized he just felt he hadn't quite done his duty if he didn't ask about her school record.

After placing them in the capable hands of the Mitsuis, I thought my responsibility was ended. But to my surprise, I had a telephone call from Mrs. Mitsui telling me she had found the ideal solution for their wedding. They could have it in the Kyoto YWCA with me as the minister to perform the ceremony since both of them knew me. I was a bit taken aback, as I had never performed a wedding in Japanese. Also I would have to be absent from my English Bible class at the church where I was helping the woman pastor, Mrs. Nakaue, with the young people. However, she assured me the impending wedding was important enough for me to be excused from my weekend duties. When I expressed anxiety about doing the ceremony in Japanese, both the pastor and Mrs. Mitsui assured me I could rise to the occasion. As an active member of the YWCA, Mrs. Mitsui could communicate with friends in Kyoto to make the proper arrangements. Both the YW and YM in Japan were accustomed to putting on Christian weddings at a reasonable cost. They could also cater the reception which was to be a fairly simple afternoon tea.

After I had agreed to do the ceremony, I spent a lot of time practicing reading the ritual aloud in order to become familiar with it. Another problem was about what I should wear. Up to that time, I had been teaching in the school, with an English Bible class as my only church duty. So I did not have a good ministerial robe. Fortunately just across the street from our mission house was the home of Emori San, one of the Hiroshima Maidens who had gone to America for surgery. She was much improved in her appearance, and her hands had become more flexible. She had started a dressmaking business in her home and she had already made some clothes for me. In those days seamstresses were skilled at making a perfect pattern from looking at a picture. After I showed her the picture of a robe in the Cokesbury catalog for Methodist Church equipment, she produced a beautiful robe which I am still using.

In Japanese Christian wedding ceremonies, the pastor always reads the entire 13th chapter of I Corinthians, which we call the "love chapter" in the New Testament. When I expressed some anxiety about being able to do this well enough, the groom assured me no one would understand it anyway, since most of the people there would be non-Christians with no knowledge of the Bible.

The women at the YWCA had arranged the room with a Japanese flower arrangement on the altar, with a simple gold screen behind it. There was a reed organ on which one of Nobuko's friends played the wedding march. So there I was, on their wedding day, reading the ceremony in Japanese before a roomful of friends and relatives of the bride and groom. At the reception, there were the usual speeches by the parents, teachers, and friends of the couple. It did my heart good to hear Nobuko's non-Christian father comment on the chapter in Corinthians I had read: "I really liked those beautiful words Miss Hartman read from the Bible. I would like to go to a quiet place and read them again, and reflect on their meaning." I felt rather smug as I remembered what Akihiro had said about no one understanding them.

Their marriage was certainly a good example of a so-called arranged marriage turning into a love marriage. They seemed to be very happy whenever I visited them. I received the announcement of the birth of their first child within a year or two, and they were ecstatic to have a healthy boy. They sent me pictures of their happy family from time to time. So I was shocked to receive a telegram when the baby was only 10 months old, telling of his sudden death from pneumonia. It seemed to have been diagnosed too late, and even though they administered oxygen, they couldn't save him.

I was made aware again that they really considered me as their go-between to whom they looked when problems arose. I felt very helpless to do anything except to telephone them, and later to write, assuring them I would be remembering them in my prayers.

When I visited them at the time of our spring conference, they told me they had bought a small piece of land to build a new house. Nobuko couldn't bear to stay in the house with so many sad memories. The architect husband of one of her classmates had made the plans. It turned out to be a lovely house which won an architectural prize. By the time their house was built, they were expecting a new baby.

It so happened I was visiting them when the second baby was born. Akihiro had planned to take me sightseeing to a nearby island. Nobuko assured us she would be fine even though her time was getting near. To our surprise, when we came back in the late afternoon, a neighbor told us she was in the local hospital and their baby daughter had already been born. It was rather a shock for Akihiro to get used to having a baby girl, as he seemed to have been sure it would be another boy. He invited me to go with him to the hospital, and since small hospitals in Japan were run more casually than our American ones, they let us both go in to see the mother and the baby. Both seemed to be doing fine, and Nobuko was full of happiness. In a few years they did have a boy which pleased them both. Through the years I watched the children grow and become strong young people.

Unfortunately their happiness was cut off when Nobuko was in her early forties, and the children were in their early teens. She developed cancer of the stomach. Most Japanese doctors at that time thought it best not to tell the patient she had cancer. She was in and out of the hospital for a year or so. I was able to visit her at the hospital on my way home for retirement. She looked thin and weak, but she still had her usual smile. She seemed to feel she could leave the hospital soon. She must have had an idea that it was getting worse instead of better, but she tried not to lose hope. I heard of her death not long after I had returned home, and I telephoned Akihiro immediately. It was a very difficult time for all of them, but Nobuko's mother who lived nearby, helped out with the children as much as she could.

After a short time, he wrote me to explain that he felt he could not bring up a teen-age daughter by himself, and he was marrying another Christian woman who had been a colleague of Nobuko's at the school where she taught. So the children and Nobuko's parents knew her as a friend of the family. She was also a Hiroshima girl who had gone to the same church with Nobuko. She remembered me from the English Bible class.

When I went back to Japan in 1986, they urged me to visit them. I was rather surprised when they took me to visit Nobuko's grave with them. We sang one of her favorite hymns and had a prayer together. Kimie, the new wife, took flowers to place on the grave. She seemed to take this in stride, as she loved Nobuko as a good friend, and wished to remember her. I am sure it wasn't easy to bring up two children in their difficult teen years who were still mourning their mother. She seems to have done a good job and she makes Akihiro a good wife. When I visited in 1992, she took me to the grave again, with fresh flowers. When I had visited before, the children were too shy to say much to me at mealtime, either in Japanese or English. But I was pleased they had matured so much and they seemed to enjoy telling me about themselves the last time I went.

At the time of the death of their baby, and later at Nobuko's death, it crossed my mind that the parents of the couple might have wondered if having a Christian wedding had brought them bad luck. Nothing like that had ever been expressed, but I wondered if they might have thought that. To my surprise, a mutual friend who attended Nobuko's church, wrote me not so long after her death to tell me that her mother had become a Christian and was now a member of that church. I was also pleased to find that Nobuko's mother continued to be a part of the family, and she seemed to get along well with Kimie. When I visited them the last time, they invited her to have dinner with the family while I was there.

The latest chapter in this story is that their son, Tadashi, wrote to ask if he could visit me when he comes to America along with college friends on a holiday trip. I was pleased that he felt free to write me, and I sent him an invitation to come. Evidently he has been brought up with the idea of me as the go-between of his parents' marriage who will always be a part of the family.

21. The Turning Point

From the time when I came back to Hiroshima to begin my work as a full time missionary, I made it a point to attend monthly meetings of the Kyodan clergy in the city. By that time I could understand most of what was being said. My hope was to let them know that my new role was not just teaching English at the school. I wanted them to know my willingness to work with Sunday school teachers and to have more connection between our school and the churches. It took quite awhile to get on their mailing list. I had to take the initiative in finding out when the meetings would be held. I was not at all sure they wanted me to come. But I felt it was important to try to keep the school and the church activities correlated when possible. It came as a surprise to me when the chairman of the pastors' group told another missionary how much they appreciated my attendance at these meetings.

That was an example of the difficulty of having good communication with the pastors. After much effort, I was able to set up a leadership training course for church school teachers in the city. Our young J-3 music teacher, Eva Saito, worked with me to plan it. She provided musical training and we enlisted other Japanese teachers to lead some of the courses. We found the Sunday school teachers eager to learn more about creative teaching methods.

In spite of some good response to my extra-curricular work at the school, I felt a good deal of frustration because these groups were canceled so frequently. When exam time came around, students felt they had to eliminate all extras and intensify their study. There were also many holidays which happened to fall on the day of one of my weekly after-school classes. That meant missing out for a whole week. When they prepared for the big autumn field day (undokai), the physical education teacher required many after-school practices which wiped out my classes. As a result, I had a tendency to take on more English classes in the curriculum. I felt guilty to have so much free time while others were overloaded. So gradually I was taking on the same role I had as a J-3.

I tried to express some of this feeling in my annual reports I sent to the mission board in New York. I indicated that my work was experimental as I was trying to carve out a new place for myself in the school. I mentioned my concern that I had to compete for the time of these students who had such busy schedules. I wondered if there might be a need in some rural area where young people had no contact with a missionary. I had some vague hope that the mission board might respond by suggesting a place where I could do more direct work with churches. I suppose someone read those reports, but I never had any feedback from anyone. My other vague hope was that local pastors would take some initiative in suggesting that I might work more directly with their Christian education programs after our successful leadership course. But the longer I lived in Japan, the more I realized things do not work that way in their culture. None of the pastors would dare to confront our strong-minded president, Miss Hirose, to suggest pulling me out of the school.

After returning from my 1963 furlough when I had completed my divinity degree in Union Seminary, I began to think seriously about how I could leave full time teaching in the school and initiate some kind of direct work with the churches. One of my dreams was to become a district worker who could help in training Sunday school teachers in the Kyodan churches of the city. I had visited enough church schools to realize that their main method was to gather the children of all ages together and give them a watered-down sermon. Usually the minister or the superintendent took on that task. Many of the teachers were young people who were fairly new Christians. I think the pastors didn't quite trust them to be able to teach the true message of the Bible to the children. By the time the opening assembly was over, only a small fragment of time was left for meeting in various age groups. My hope was to give the teachers more confidence and more understanding of how children learn. I believe that children learn more by working together in meaningful activities than by listening to sermons.

But when I suggested such a position, I found the pastors did not see a need for that kind of work.

They did feel a need for someone to help in gathering new churches in areas where none existed. One of the older ministers, Mr. Yamashiro, who was easy for me to talk to, suggested that if I helped to start a new church, I could create a Sunday school to serve as a model for other churches. In addition to his encouragement, one of the J-3s, Sonja Hedlund, helped me to make the break. She was a very outgoing person who related well to people and she was not afraid to try new things. Her enthusiasm was infectious, and she spurred me on to take more initiative in changing my work.

However, after I made my decision, it was a very slow process to make the change. I assumed the first step would be to talk to the moderator of our district who was one of the local pastors. He was a particularly taciturn man with whom it was hard to communicate. He did not give me a "yes" or "no" answer, but I assumed he would bring it up to the other pastors. When I found that nothing happened, I confided in Mr. Yamashiro again. He told me the other pastors also found it hard to communicate with this man. He suggested I make an appointment with the chair of evangelism, Mr. Fujita, whom I knew fairly well.

When I approached him about doing pioneer evangelism in the area north of the city, he agreed there was a need for a new church, as widespread development was taking place there. For the first time in my experience, Japanese people were affluent enough to take on a mortgage and build their own homes. Bulldozers came in to terrace the surrounding hillsides, and water and sewage lines were laid. They sold small plots of land lined up side by side on the flat places. Mr. Fujita's church in Ushita was the nearest one to that area. But he said new people were not so likely to take a 30 minute bus ride to find a church.

After that encouraging beginning, he began to lay out all the negative points of doing this work. He pointed out that there were already some very weak "dendoshos" (preaching points) in our district which had never grown into a church. They just limped along with a few Christians meeting in a home with a part-time pastor. He was emphatic in saying we didn't need any more of those. This new housing development did seem to present a good possibility for success, but he said even Japanese pastors found it very hard to gather a new church, and all churches in Japan grow very slowly. He said it would be even harder for a non-Japanese to make headway in such work. By the time he had painted this negative picture, I had just about decided he was telling me I should give up the whole idea.

But suddenly he surprised me by saying: "But Miss Hartman, if you do take this on, I don't want you to give up when it is just partly formed. I want you to keep at it until it really becomes a church."

Then it dawned on me that he had been testing me to see if this was some kind of visionary whim or whether I was truly serious enough and would have enough persistence to face such difficulties and carry it through. Once we got to that point, he was very helpful in suggesting two of his own church members in that area who could help me. One was Mrs. Kawagoe, a home economics teacher in our college who was already a good friend. The other was Mrs. Fujisaki, an English teacher who would be helpful if I wished to translate Sunday school materials into Japanese. His attitude was more generous than some of the other pastors who made a point of saying this church should try for new members rather than expecting those from other churches to transfer, even if they lived in the area. Mr. Fujita's earthy way of expressing it was that the only way to get baby squirrels is from parent squirrels. So he didn't oppose members who might wish to transfer from his church to the new one.

Our high school chaplain, Mr. Fujikawa and his wife who lived in that part of town, had always hoped I might be able to use my theological training in some more direct way. When it was decided I would be assigned to their area, they were eager to help me. Mrs. Fujikawa took me to see various houses for rent, but most of the new houses were cut up into such small rooms, it would be hard to have enough space for church services. Mr. Fujikawa volunteered to be my co-pastor, and that proved to be a godsend in starting the work. His wife offered to do my secretarial work. They had no children, and she was fairly good in English. I could tell her what I wanted to say in a letter, and she could put it into good Japanese.

As it turned out, Mrs. Kawagoe was the one who found a suitable house to rent in the town of Furuichi, not far from the growing edge of the city. It was in a newly built group of row houses on a plot where there was formerly a truck garden. Mine was on the corner, and it was somewhat larger than the others, as the landlord planned it for her brother who later decided not to live there. It was the only one we found which had two rooms upstairs that could be opened into one room when the sliding doors were removed.

My next step was to confront Miss Hirose to tell her I wished to leave full time teaching at the school. I dreaded having to do that, and as I expected, she did not look favorably on my decision. She warned me of the difficulties of gathering a new church. Of course she knew she couldn't force me to stay. I told her I would continue the two hours of English Bible in the college curriculum, as I knew it was important to have as many teachers with Masters degrees as possible to keep up their status with the Ministry of Education.

One pleasant surprise occurred when I went to look at the new house. When a next door neighbor heard my voice, she remarked, "That sounds like Miss Hartman." When she came over to greet me, I discovered she was the wife of Mr. Matsufuji, one of the Jo Gakuin English teachers. They seemed pleased to have me for a neighbor, although they wondered if I would be able to adjust to this simple Japanese house. Having this Christian couple beside me proved to be providential, as they were very supportive. After I moved in, Mrs. Matsufuji offered to go with me to the door of each of the neighbors to give the customary gift of a newcomer. People usually gave soap, or matches or sugar or some other staple to each household in the nearest group of houses. I would give to each one my speech which I had memorized in Japanese: "My name is Doris Hartman and I am your new neighbor. 'Dozo Yoroshiku.'" (This Japanese phrase might be freely translated as, "Please be kind to me.") Later she also walked around the area with me to visit homes where there were children whom we invited to our new church school which was to meet on Saturday afternoons.

So, in 1966, I had finally been able to become part of a Japanese neighborhood and to launch a new venture purely on faith. Even though I had struggled to begin this new chapter in my life, I wondered if I would be able to overcome all the obstacles. It was a totally unknown situation where I had set myself to start a new church from scratch. Certainly I had been warned about the difficulties. Would anyone come to our services? Would I be able to operate in Japanese instead of being surrounded by English speaking people? I felt a little bit like Abraham who started out without knowing where God was leading him. But so far God had provided the support of Mr. Fujikawa as my co-pastor and the Matsufujis as my supportive next-door neighbors, as well as the sponsoring committee who agreed to work with me on this difficult process of gathering a church. So that gave me the courage to step out on faith to see where God would lead me.

22. Life In Furuichi

As I sat immersed in hot water up to my neck in the old-fashioned Japanese bathtub in my small row house, my feelings were mixed. I felt a surge of joy that I had finally managed to get into a situation with new possibilities. Having broken from the routine of teaching English to junior and senior high girls, I was now free to embark on an adventure of pioneer evangelism along with our chaplain, Mr. Fujikawa. We were going to try to gather a church in an outlying area where there had been none. At the same time, I wondered how I ever had the audacity to think I would be able to carry out such a project. In this strongly Buddhist society where the church had been planted more than 100 years ago, it was still very slow going for Christian pastors and missionaries to make headway in gathering a church.

The members of Shujo Church where I had an English Bible class were very helpful in moving me to the new house in Furuichi. Some of the women helped to clean the kitchen. A high school boy from my class used his father's pick-up truck to move my things. His family gave me a discount on futons and floor cushions from their cotton factory. Mrs. Nakaue, the pastor, presented me with folding tables for the sanctuary. I was moved when a carpenter from the church offered to build shelves in the deep kitchen cupboard to make it more useful. Because of a bronchial cancer operation, he was unable to talk. When I asked for his bill he wrote in Japanese: "This is my contribution to your project."

After I moved into my small Japanese house, my whole way of living went through a major change. During my first fourteen years I had lived in a Western style house where we had two maids as helpers. Our house was not luxurious by American standards, but in the early years when most of the Japanese were relatively poor, it seemed rather upscale. We slept on beds and we wore our shoes in the house. We had a space oil heater in the living room with small gas stoves in our bedrooms. Our bathroom had a Western style bathtub and toilet with a large hot water heater in the laundry room to provide hot water for the whole house.

Except for the few months when Joy, the young home economics teacher and I lived in the Japanese house in Ushita, I had always been on the school campus where we related mostly to people connected with the school. In contrast, my house in Furuichi was set in the midst of many small houses in what was originally a country town. It used to have many truck gardens to supply produce to the city of Hiroshima. But in recent years it had become a bedroom town, as it was only 30 minutes from the city by bus. We approached my house by walking down a narrow alley just beside the big agriculture co-op building located right on the bus road. We placed a signboard at the beginning of the alley to point to our house church. A narrow walkway separated my house and the other two row houses from the back of the large co-op building. That space was used for storing fuel, for garbage pails, and for children's tricycles and various toys. On hot summer days, my next door neighbor put out a small rubber pool in which her little boy and the twins in the next house could spend time cooling off. The only real play space they had was in the courtyard of the old Shinto shrine just behind our group of houses.

We entered the house by sliding doors to a small entry way called the "genkan." There was a wooden chest with sliding wooden doors for storing shoes, and the slippers needed for guests. Here we took off our shoes, leaving all the sand and dirt on the cement floor. Japanese people taught me to line up shoes so they would be ready to step into when leaving the house. When we stepped up to the wooden floor of the hallway we could wear slippers and also on the tiled floor of the kitchen. But the living room and bedrooms had "tatami" floors made of woven grass matting stretched on wooden panels. Even slippers were not allowed on these floors as that might damage the surface.

Immediately to the right of the entry way was the Japanese style toilet. Although we would call it an outhouse, it was attached to the house, with a metal cover on the cement base outside.

Periodically, a small tank truck came into our alley and inserted its long hose to vacuum out the contents of the toilet. One thing I dreaded was having the vacuum truck come when I had a meeting in progress. If they were adults, they pretended not to notice, but children were more uninhibited. They were likely to hold their noses and to exclaim, "It stinks." The new housing developments all have flush toilets, but in old sections of town where no sewage system is installed, one needs a septic tank which is very costly and takes up needed space.

To the left of the kitchen at the front of the house was the bathroom where there was a sink and a round metal tub sunk into a tile rim. The tile floor had a drain, as the method of bathing is to wash outside the tub before soaking. Each evening I filled the tub with cold water using a hose attached to the faucet in the sink. Then I kindled a fire in the small fire box just to the left of my front door. Since I was the only one to use it, I didn't need to refill the tub every day. I could just build a fire again to heat the same water for a few days.

The kitchen was on the left of the entry way, just behind the bathroom. There was a stainless steel sink with a cold water faucet located under a window, but the only view was the alley and my next door neighbor's house. Although I couldn't see into their bathroom, I could hear the husband do his routine gargling every morning before he went to work. That helped me to know whether I was behind schedule or not.

To the right of the sink was a two burner hot plate fueled by propane gas, fed by two tanks behind my house. The only shelf space was a swinging shelf on the wall to the left of the sink for staple foods where I had a curtain made to hide the clutter. Later I designed a set of shelves for dishes which another carpenter made and fastened to the wall above my table. There was room for a kitchen table and chairs. I even managed to entertain two guests by pulling out the table leaves. When I had more than two, we had to use the living room, or sometimes the upstairs space.

At the back of the house was my living room where I walked only in stocking feet. Large floor length windows opened to the narrow space between my house and the roadway, where I hung my laundry. In order to have some storage space, I had a carpenter make an upright wooden shed using only the space between the edge of the house and the windows. On the right wall of the living room was one of the large deep cupboards for bedding. Between that cupboard and the window was a narrow clothes closet with two drawers underneath for storing towels and sheets. I had my desk and files and bookcases in that room. My plan was to live in this downstairs part and use the upstairs only for church and Sunday school. But after a short time, I began to experience aching knees when I climbed the stairs. I noticed that the linens in those drawers near the floor were always damp. The floor was just a few feet from the ground beneath, as there was no basement. Whenever I lay down, I could feel the vibrations when a motor scooter drove down the alley which wrapped around my house. So I tried taking my futon upstairs and sleeping there where the sun came in the windows and helped to dry out the dampness. I noticed an improvement in my knees right away. I still used the downstairs for a dressing room, but I kept all my bedding in the upstairs closet.

By removing the sliding doors, we could make the upstairs into a fairly good sized room for church services. I had a carpenter put dividing shelves into the cupboard in the front room upstairs where we could keep toys and other materials for our pre-school group at our church school. We had a pump organ which I had received from our school. It had been purchased with mission board money when our J-3 music teacher used it to give organ lessons to local church organists who wanted to improve their skills. It was too wide to be taken up the stairway, but the workmen brought it on a truck and lifted it by ropes through the wide upstairs windows. Later we had a lectern and an altar made to fit under the windows at the front of the house. During church services, we sat on floor cushions with folding tables on which to place our Bibles and hymnbooks.

One other improvement I made almost immediately was to have a sturdy railing built at the side of the narrow stairway which everyone had to use. Later when my next door neighbor's little boy fell all the way down their stairs, the husband came to look at my railing as he wished to install one like it.

There was no room for a live-in maid even if I had wanted one. By that time, in 1966, it was much easier to do the shopping. Just down the street was a fairly large super market with good fresh vegetables and fruit and staple food as well as a fish counter. There was also a very good meat market and a fish market nearer my house. If I needed imported food, it was easy to find almost anything in the city department stores, and we could get very good bread and pastry at Andersen's bakery.

I did find a cleaning woman who could come in twice a week. She hung my bedding out the window on sunny days to air it out. She also took my laundry home to use her electric washer as I didn't have one. Since I had only a broom, she began bringing her electric sweeper once a week to clean more thoroughly. After a short time, I felt embarrassed enough to get my own sweeper. I never bought a washer, as I had no room for one. Sometimes I built the fire for the bath, but my cleaning woman could do it so much faster than I, that we agreed for her to stop by on her way to do her afternoon shopping. Even though she started the fire at about 5:00 o'clock, the water was still very hot even if I didn't use it until midnight. That was the advantage of the old-fashioned metal tub.

As a way of becoming known in the neighborhood, our committee suggested having evening classes in oral English for children and adults. We charged a nominal fee to be put into a building fund for the church we hoped to build some day. These classes were highly successful. With a minimum amount of advertising, we were able to fill up four levels of English which I offered on Thursday and Friday evenings. There was a half hour class for elementary children, with an hour for junior high students who were just beginning to study English in school. After supper, I taught senior high students for an hour. Then on Friday I had an adult class of college students and working people.

Since I had three English classes on Thursday evening, I had a problem about managing to prepare and eat supper that evening.

During the years I found neighbors who would bring me a tray of the same food as they cooked for their family. Of course I paid them for it. My next arrangement was with a pleasant grandmother who lived nearby in one of the more pretentious old houses. I wouldn't have dared to ask her, but she had helped Mrs. Kawagoe when her husband was bedridden for a short time, and she seemed to enjoy doing it. She and her adopted daughter did not get along well together, and she wasn't allowed to do anything in the kitchen. She had a big garden which she enjoyed working in. When I approached her about providing a meal on Thursday, she seemed pleased. But she warned me her cooking would be from the Meiji era (the late 1800's). I assured her any kind of food would be fine. She agreed to let me pay for the food, but often she brought fresh vegetables from her garden for which she refused any payment. She always arrived unobtrusively while I was upstairs with the children. When I came downstairs, the hot dishes were covered and everything was attractively set on my table. Later when I was having my last class, she slipped in to do the dishes, always leaving the sink beautifully scoured.

I was very sorry when she decided to leave her unhappy situation and enter a retirement center in another province. Mrs. Fujikawa and I drove over to visit her once after she moved. She seemed to be happy there, although I wondered how she could adjust to living in one small room after being used to her large Japanese house. She did have a small garden where she could have fun raising vegetables. She had never attended our church, but she seemed to like receiving the Christian news sheet which we sent out to shut-ins each month. She always wrote a letter to thank me for it.

My Fridays were rather tightly scheduled also. In the morning, Mrs. Harano came to go over my sermon for the following Sunday. I wondered if she would want to take the long bus ride out to Furuichi when I moved. But she enjoyed the ride and she said she liked having this change. At that time she was living with her son who was a French professor in the city university. So she didn't have household duties. I always prepared a light lunch for us to share after our morning's work, as we often continued into the afternoon.

I was glad for the custom in Japanese Protestant churches of having a lay person lead the service, taking charge of all the ritual, leaving only the sermon and the benediction for the pastor. I had to have my sermon fairly well worked out before she arrived at about 9:00 A.M. I usually typed it out in English, but I tried to put it into Japanese before she came. Or else I "talked" it to her in Japanese, and she helped me correct mistakes and polish it up.

In the evening I had an adult English class. There were times when I had someone to help with my Friday evening meal also. During one period, Nobuko Miyake, who was a senior in our college offered to provide a box lunch for me in order to have time to talk with me, before our English class began. She lived with her grandmother who was a wonderful cook. She always brought a tasty meal. Nobuko had become a Christian in her junior high years. It was a Pentecostal type of church and as she matured, she found it too noisy and not intellectual enough for her. Then for a time she attended a Reformed church which seemed to be more Calvinistic than Calvin. When she joined my English Bible class at our college, she said once, "Miss Hartman, your God and Miss McMillan's God are quite different from the God in our church." They stressed preparing for heaven, and they didn't seem to expect much pleasure here on earth. They had very strict rules about arriving on time and not being absent without a good reason.

As her home was on the bus route to our Furuichi Church, she eventually decided to become a member of our church. She made a real contribution by being the leader of our junior high group. She had a sunny disposition and a very enthusiastic faith. The young people all loved her.

She did her senior thesis at our college in English, although they had a choice of doing it in Japanese if they preferred. A visiting professor from America was so impressed with what she wrote, that he predicted she would become the Georgia Harkness of Japan. She was a well known theologian in the Methodist

Church, who wrote several books on theology and some poetry. Although Nobuko had never heard of her, when she found I had some of her books, she eagerly read them all.

I think our time together did serve a purpose. In order to become more fluent in English, she often went to the Christian center at the nearby American military base where she made friends with some of the GI's. As she was quite naive about boy friends, she tended to fall in love with each one. Once I was able to persuade her that it would not be a good idea to go on a weekend trip with one of these young men. Later she received a scholarship to study theology in America and she is now an ordained United Methodist minister serving a Japanese-American church in Denver. She has won several awards for her outstanding work as a minister. She showed excellent judgment in choosing a husband, an American young man whom she met at a peace meeting toward the end of her graduate work. Soon after my retirement, she asked me to officiate at their wedding in Pennsylvania along with the bridegroom's pastor brother. When I visited her church once, she told her congregation that I had been her role model which helped her to decide to enter the ministry.

Many college students and other young adults from our English classes came also to a Sunday morning English Bible class, during the years when we had our worship on Sunday evening. They formed the custom of staying after class for sociability and discussion of problems. They could slip down to the grocery store near my house to buy a bottle of milk and some buns for their lunch. On some Sundays the girls asked me to give them a cooking lesson in the afternoon. People were just beginning to buy small ovens, and they wished to learn how to make cookies and cakes. Once or twice a year we had recreational outings. At Christmas we usually hiked to a nearby hillside to cut a Christmas tree on land owned by one of our adult members.

When I first moved to Furuichi, I had no schedule except Wednesday afternoons when I went to our college to teach the Bible in English to sophomores who were taking an English major. I always stayed after class to have an informal English

Bible class for girls who wanted to have an extra hour of Bible study, hymn singing, and discussion. Many of those students continued in that class during their four years.

Gradually the other days of the week became full, though I tried to keep Monday as my day off. We started a parenting class led by a volunteer retired social worker. This seemed to fill a need with the parents of our church school children. Most of them were no longer living in extended families, and they welcomed a chance to ask questions about bringing up their children.

After I returned from my first furlough, the members requested that we have our worship on Sunday mornings. That meant preparing a sermon in Japanese every Sunday except the one when Mr. Fujikawa preached. So I took the leap of faith that I would be up to this new challenge. We still were able to call on some of the lay people occasionally to preach. Somehow I managed to rise to the occasion, in spite of my doubts.

Living in a church meant having some people with problems who came to ask for help. Usually these people were in need of money, and it was difficult to know if their stories were true, or if they thought that a church was a place where they could make a "soft touch." I remember one man who came to ask for money to take a train to his old home in Kyushu. He told me he had been in jail, but while he was there, he had become a Christian, and he really wanted to make a new start. If he could only get to his home town in Kyushu, he could have a job in his family's apple orchard. As a pledge that he would pay the money back, he left a bag of golf clubs with me. My feeling was that it was better to err on the side of compassion than to turn him away. But I realized afterward it would have been better if I had taken him to the station to buy a train ticket. When I told Mr. Fujikawa about this man, he was very skeptical. He said he had heard many ex-convicts who claimed to have become Christian, since they knew that the minister would be sympathetic. He also informed me that prisoners are always given enough money to reach their home town when they are freed. Well, he proved to be right, as I never heard from the man again. When the man never showed up to claim them, I took the golf clubs to the small police box in our village. They were not willing to take them off my hands and they had no way to find out where they might have been stolen from. Finally I gave them to my carpenter friend who liked to play golf, but I warned him they were probably stolen property.

I never regretted my decision to leave the somewhat sheltered life at the school to embark on the adventure of gathering a church. At last I could become a part of a Japanese neighborhood. The work was challenging and it caused me to stretch my abilities to the limit. It strengthened my faith that when we are willing to take the first step, God will open many new doors, enabling us to accomplish more than we ever thought possible.

23. Gathering A Church

My new venture was surely a fulfillment of that old proverb, "Fools rush in where angels fear to tread." Probably Mr. Fujikawa realized that when he offered to be my co-pastor. As the work progressed, I began to see how important it was to have him and his wife as my co-workers. When I took on this assignment, I had a rather vague picture of how to go about it. I knew there were graduates of our school in this area. So I thought there might be some of them who would be interested in coming to a Bible study group. I also thought of trying to start some kind of mothers' chorus, as such groups were popular in Japanese communities. Japanese people love to sing and even non-Christians know some hymns and oratorios. Membership in such a group might guide them into the nearest church congregation.

However, when I was assigned to Furuichi, I realized there was no church nearby. The ministers wanted me to be the pastor of this group we would be gathering. From the beginning, I knew I needed the help of Christians living in the area. My first step was to form a sponsoring committee who would give guidance in procedure. In addition to the Fujikawas, I asked my neighbors, the Matsufujis, and the two women from Mr. Fujita's church whom he had suggested. Everyone agreed that I should also ask Mrs. Harada, a strong Christian woman in the next town who had left her church because of a disagreement with the pastor. She was active in the city-wide church women's group. I remembered being impressed by a talk she had made. She explained that a Christian can express her faith in community service as well as by attending church on Sundays. She told some of her experiences in the school PTA where she had served as a mediator when there was a dispute over a new building.

Mrs. Fujikawa and I made an appointment to invite her to join our committee. I was surprised and pleased at her eager response. She told us she had been praying for nine years that a church could be started in her neighborhood. She welcomed us as an answer to her prayers. She told us her reason for leaving her former church which was located in a different part of the city from her present home. The pastor had decided to build a new sanctuary in a different part of the city in order to enlarge the kindergarten. She felt he was ignoring the wishes of those who had sacrificed to build a church on that particular site to serve that neighborhood. She felt that the kindergarten existed for the church, and not the church for the kindergarten. Many churches in Japan started weekday kindergartens as a way of serving the families in the neighborhood. But they soon saw the income as a supplement to the minister's salary in small struggling churches. Usually the minister's wife was trained as a kindergarten teacher, but the minister became the official director which added to his salary.

After she left her church, the young assistant minister came to Mrs. Harada's house every week to lead a Bible study group to which she invited many of her neighbors. The Ibuchi family who lived next door were also members of that church. His mother had been one of the original founders. So he also objected strongly to having the minister pull up stakes and move to another part of the city. Mrs. Harada not only became a charter member of our church; she also contributed a large sum of money since she had been accumulating her tithes in the hope of starting a new church. She also was willing to take her turn as a lay preacher at our services. Everyone appreciated her down-to-earth sermons which concentrated on living your faith in daily life. Eventually Mr. and Mrs. Ibuchi also transferred their membership to our new church.

Our committee decided to begin by having our services on Sunday night. That would enable those who attended churches in the city to go to their own service in the morning. But they could invite neighbors to come with them to our service at night. I had enough experience in preparing talks in Japanese to realize that I couldn't preach every Sunday at the beginning. I agreed to preach once a month and Mr. Fujikawa would preach once. Then we could invite pastors from Kyodan churches in the city to preach on the other Sundays. Some of the members of the committee also agreed to take a turn at being the lay preacher.

As I explained earlier, the moderator was so uncommunicative that he had not informed the other pastors about this new preaching point. So it came as somewhat of a shock when they heard all this had been decided without their being consulted. But they all agreed there was a need for a preaching point in that growing edge of the city. When they got used to the idea, they were very cooperative in taking their turn at preaching. This was helpful in enabling them to have a part in the project.

When I first moved out to Furuichi, I sent out invitations to all the graduates of our school who lived in that part of town, to come for an afternoon tea. Since I had taught in the school for about 14 years, there were many who would know me, and I assumed they would respond to such an invitation. Since I didn't have enough teacups, I borrowed some from my neighbor, Mrs. Matsufuji. Then I baked enough cookies to take care of the number of people I had invited. Imagine how shocked I was when only one woman showed up! But it turned out to be worthwhile to get to know her. She was a pre-war graduate who had not had much social life in recent years because of health problems. When my invitation came, she felt ready to have some social life again, and she had very warm feelings about her alma mater. We had a good visit and I invited her to bring her preschool daughter to our Saturday church school. She was willing to help Mrs. Matsufuji with the pre-school class. She remained a good friend, though she never joined our church.

When I tried to evaluate this dismal failure, I realized I had forgotten what I should have known from my years in Japan. People act in groups, and my procedure should have been to talk to some of the graduates I knew and suggest they invite their friends. No one wants to stand out alone, and since they didn't know who else might be coming, they just stayed home.

One of my hopes was to try to build up a model church school in this new project. I was fortunate in persuading the young woman chaplain at our college, who had just earned a Master's degree in Christian education from Oberlin Seminary to help us start our church school. We decided to have it on Saturday afternoons, as children went to school on Saturday morning, but they were free in the afternoon. That would give us more time than if they met Sunday morning before church. Our other reason was being able to get volunteers from other churches to help with the teaching.

Soon after I moved into the house, a young housewife with a small child on her back, and another one in tow, came to offer her help in our new church. Her husband's uncle, who was the principal at Jo Gakuin High School, had urged her to meet me. She and her husband were members of the Episcopal Church in the city, but she found it hard to take her small children on the bus each Sunday. She volunteered to be our organist as she was an excellent musician. Eventually she also served as one of the pre-school teachers.

Another young housewife came with her two elementary school children to enroll in our Saturday school. They had heard about it from some of the neighborhood children. She told me she had been baptized as a high school girl in her hometown in Kyushu, but she hadn't attended church since she married and had family responsibilities. Although I could see she was reluctant at first, I persuaded her to become the teacher of our primary class. She did an excellent job for many years. Mrs. Matsufuji agreed to take a pre-school class, and Mrs. Fujikawa taught the older children. The daughter of the pastor of Shujo Church where I had been teaching a Bible class, volunteered to drive out each Saturday to help us even though she taught at their Sunday church school as well as their weekday kindergarten. Ironically, after we had our staff in place, the young college chaplain realized it would be impossible for her to give the time to do this work in addition to her responsibilities at the college. She had served, however, as a catalyst to get our church school started. I might not have had the courage to do it without her. Eventually Mrs. Fujikawa became our superintendent and she proved to be a dedicated and conscientious leader.

From the beginning, our church school attracted many children from the neighborhood. Japanese parents are eager for their children to have any kind of education that is being offered. Most of them respect Christians as people who have high moral standards. So even though they are not Christian, they believe their children might get some good training to help them be better behaved. At first we had quite a turnover, as some children came out of curiosity because I was a foreigner. They knew that I taught a little English to each class--mostly in the form of songs. But gradually we built up a core of regular pupils who came every week.

Saturday became a very full day for me. The pre-school children met in the afternoon from 1:30 to 2:30 when they could have the whole upstairs for their activities. Then the older children met from 3:00 to 4:00 or 4:30. Naturally they took up the whole house as one class had to meet in my downstairs living room, while two other groups used the upstairs rooms. My only responsibility was to teach simple English songs to each group before their class time.

I tried to make our monthly teachers' meetings a time of leadership training. The teachers were eager to learn creative ways of teaching the children. Instead of the customary long sermons during the opening assembly, we had a brief time of singing, learning the Bible verse of the day and a prayer. That gave them a block of time for the classes when they were divided by age groups.

Within a few years, almost all the church schoolteachers had transferred their membership to our new church. So we no longer had to depend on volunteers from other churches. They enjoyed occasional outings when we climbed a mountain or had a picnic at some beauty spot, which helped to build a strong fellowship among them. They were also quite willing to engage in serious study of the Bible and new teaching methods.

We had outings for the children in the spring and fall. We usually went to a park or some place where there was enough space to run and play games. Our little house church had no grounds around it, and we wanted them to be able to stretch out once in awhile. During the summer we could rent a Lutheran camp site along a river just a few miles outside the city. We had a vacation Bible camp with an overnight stay. We usually had two days of classes, recreation, and a campfire service, ending with a closing worship in their chapel which seemed more like a real church than our little upstairs room.

One of the ways of gathering new members was to have home meetings. Church members would invite neighbors to join in a time of singing and Bible study, and then light refreshments. We had two daytime groups and one evening meeting, in different sections of our area. We met at the home of Mrs. Fujisaki in the adjoining town of Gion. There we discovered an elderly grandmother who was delighted to find a church which she could attend. She had been baptized in her youth in the southernmost town of Kagoshima. Since coming to live with her adopted son, she hadn't been able to attend church. But she could get to our house church by a short bus ride and she soon became one of our loyal members. When she entered the room, her sunny smile made everyone feel good.

It was hard to believe she had experienced so much tragedy in her life. After having a baby daughter, she discovered her husband who was in the navy had what they called a "second wife" in one of his ports. She took the momentous step of divorcing him though women were expected to grin and bear it, even if they knew the husband was unfaithful. In order to support herself and her daughter, she took a correspondence course in midwifery. How she managed to take enough classes to get the certificate, I am not sure. But for many years she traveled through the countryside with her small daughter, delivering babies and making friends wherever she went. If the new mother had not enough time or money to prepare a layette, she would spend evenings sewing for the baby.

During World War II, her twenty-one year old daughter who happened to be in Hiroshima, was a victim of the atom bomb. She said that in order to keep her sanity, after the death of her daughter, she took up "sumie" painting with an outstanding teacher. This became a lifelong hobby and I still have several pictures she gave me. Her strong faith upheld her, and she made a new life with her adopted son, actually one of her sister's sons, who was a school superintendent. It is customary for a person without children to adopt a relative's child in their adult years in order to have someone to take care of them in their old age. She became my most faithful correspondent after I retired. My Japanese friends who read her letters to me, always admired her beautiful penmanship and her old fashioned proper language. I visited her twice when I returned to Japan, once in Kagoshima where her son had been transferred, and later on the island of Okino Erabu where her son served as school superintendent for three years. After her death a few years ago, I missed her frequent letters.

Although we had a sign indicating the location of our house church, most people who came to church were there because someone invited them, or because of their connection with Hiroshima Jo Gakuin. Without my experience as a teacher there, it would have been much more difficult to get started. People in the neighborhood were more likely to trust me because our school was respected by the people of Hiroshima. One Sunday evening, a young woman appeared at my door with a lovely bouquet of flowers from her garden. She had walked about a half mile from her farm home in the neighborhood, after hearing I was living there. She had attended my Bible class while she was a student at our school. She had been baptized at the church in her home town of Kure. But after marrying into a non-Christian farm family, she had not been able to attend church. She was a hard-working farm wife with two children in elementary school. She showed me the card in her Bible on which I had written a Bible verse and signed my name. It seemed to be a memory she treasured. She did transfer her membership to our church. But her husband and her mother-in-law frowned on the idea of her taking time off to go to church. She brought her widowed mother who clerked at the grocery story just down the street, along with the woman who ran the store. They never became members but they attended our evening services fairly often. I called on this young woman regularly and she sometimes came to our women's group. When I returned from America in 1986, I was pleased to see her in the congregation when I preached at the 20th anniversary of our church.

Our most difficult problem was always the dynamics of human relations. In a non-Christian country, people are likely to have a rather idealistic picture of Christians, and when they meet someone who doesn't live up to these standards, they are disillusioned. One of our new members proved to be a gossip who spread stories about other members which hurt their feelings. I felt it was because of her that two of our so-called "seekers" stopped coming.

During the first year, we had a preparatory class for three or four people who expressed an interest in becoming baptized members. I asked Pastor Fujita to conduct the training class, as I was sure he could meet the needs of these people better than I could. He knew what was important to discuss with people who had no church background. At least four young women who were graduates of our college were baptized during the first few years. One of them, who was in her middle thirties, told me she had not been much interested in the chapel or the Bible study while she was a student. But later when her marriage ended in divorce, she began to feel the need of a faith to provide an anchor for her life.

The other three started coming to church in their senior year at the college. As they came nearer to the time when they would be leaving our school, they began to think more seriously about the message of Christianity and their need for a faith to live by.

Another new member came at the invitation of Mrs. Harada who was her neighbor. This young woman in her mid-thirties had been through a very unhappy divorce. She and her husband had adopted a child when she found she could not have children. But when her husband became involved with another woman, he told his wife he would like a divorce, as this woman had become pregnant. The child she had come to love as her own, had to be given back to the relative from whom they had received her. She looked up to Mrs. Harada who had been her tutor during the war years, and she wanted to have that kind of strong faith to enable her to make a new life for herself. After attending church for some time, she asked to be baptized, and she became one our most loyal members.

Sometimes I received telephone calls from people who had moved to our area from Tokyo or some other large city. They looked for a Kyodan church in the phone book and called to inquire about our services. The most surprising call was from a young man named Sakoda who lived in a country village about an hour away by bus. He had been given our number since ours was the nearest Kyodan church. I assured him I would be glad to talk to him and I gave him directions to our place. When he arrived, I was rather startled to hear that he really wanted to be baptized, although he had almost never been inside a church. His story confirmed my belief that "God works in mysterious ways his wonders to perform." Since graduating from high school he had helped his father with his nursery where they planted bushes and trees. As a young adult, he had attended the village youth group.

When he discovered their main interest was in drinking and idle gossip, he decided to spend his time reading good books. One author who made a strong impression on him was Tolstoy with his high ideals of peace. He realized his ideas were grounded in the Bible. So he wanted to learn more about the teachings of Jesus. He began to listen to the Lutheran Hour every week on the radio. They gave dramatic presentations of Bible stories, and through that program he received a correspondence course on the Christian faith. Once he attended an inspirational conference for rural youth at the national YMCA camp where he heard some excellent Christian leaders. As he became more attracted to Christianity, he attended services at the Lutheran Church in Hiroshima one Sunday. It seemed rather cold and unfriendly, and no one particularly welcomed him.

In addition to the Lutheran course, he enrolled in a correspondence course from the Kyodan Church's department of newspaper evangelism. He began reading their monthly Christian magazine. For a time he thought he could be a Christian without being part of a church. But then he began to feel he was being called to be a minister so he could help rural people understand the true meaning of the Christian faith. When he wrote to a Seminary in Tokyo which specialized in rural ministry, he was told he would have to be a church member for at least a year, and be recommended by his local pastor. As I talked to him, I realized he knew more about the Bible than many long time church members did. Of course I encouraged him to attend our Sunday night services.

From that time on, he took the long bus ride every Sunday to come to church. In our small house church, he had a chance to ask questions and to become close to our members. As they knew more about him, they agreed he was truly ready for baptism. Most churches in Japan require new members to go through a course of study for several months before being baptized. Since I would be leaving for furlough in a few months, we arranged to have his baptism soon after he started coming. Then he could apply for seminary within a year. He was sure he could get his younger brother to take his place on his father's farm. His parents thought he was crazy to give up his inheritance as the oldest son to become a pastor in a foreign religion. Before I left, Mr. and Mrs. Fujikawa and I drove up to his farm home to explain the situation to his parents. I think it was helpful for them to talk to Mr. Fujikawa, and they felt reassured that he was not getting into some outlandish group. They did give their permission for him to leave the following year.

Without my asking them, the Fujikawas volunteered to live in my house while I was gone. They were devoted to our fledgling church, and they wanted to keep it from falling apart. Her mother agreed to come from Tokyo to live in their rented house during that time. Of course it was just a few miles away, and they could go home frequently. I genuinely appreciated their generous offer, as it meant some sacrifice for them. Later they told me that Mr. Sakoda often stayed overnight after the service when he could have long talks with Mr. Fujikawa to prepare him for seminary.

Before I came back, he had enrolled in the five-year course in Tsurukawa Rural Training Seminary. Fortunately he met a young kindergarten teacher who had come back to the seminary to train for the ministry. Since she graduated ahead of him, she was able to get an office job there which enabled them to get married while he was still in school. Usually Japanese weddings are very expensive as they have an elaborate dinner at a restaurant or wedding hall. But our church members arranged for a simple ceremony at our beautiful small chapel in Jo Gakuin High School. The church women provided simple refreshments to be served in one of the classrooms near the chapel. His family was impressed with the warmth of the people, and their generous reception which was so much less expensive than a traditional Japanese wedding. Even though they probably hosted another party for their relatives where drinks could be served, they appreciated what the church people did for the couple.

During the first ten years, we were able to gather about 30 members. We had an overflow crowd of church school children, and many students in our night school English classes. Our women formed a women's society and within a few years they put on a very successful church bazaar. The neighbors flocked to see our array of handwork and home baked cookies and cakes. Our women thought of this as an opportunity to let the neighbors know more about the Christian faith. They asked me to lead them in a brief time of devotion and prayer before the crowd came. Our Saturday school took a holiday, and most of them came along with some of their parents to enjoy the fun. Gradually our members began to talk about how we could embark on a new and more difficult venture--that of building a sanctuary.

I really did not think I could meet that challenge. I was hoping it could be put off until I retired. I would rather have someone else struggle with such a big undertaking. But then an unexpected turn of events caused me to be plunged into the middle of actually building a small church just down the street from where we had been meeting. Once more I was challenged to step out in faith, believing that God would provide for our needs.

24. Our Mini Church

We learned that an old beat-up glass shop just a few steps from our church was to be offered for sale. The widow-owner had been renting it to an old man for a nominal sum. He ran the shop but after he died, she decided to sell it in order to distribute her estate to her children while she was still alive. In Japan the land is measured by the "tsubo" which is equal to six square feet. In one of my letters I quoted the probable price as $520 per "tsubo." I gave an estimate of about $25,000 for that small piece of land. As I remember it, when we actually built the church, the total cost was about $40,000. People usually expect to pay more for the land than for the building.

After 10 years of saving the tuition fees from my English lessons, the amount had become fairly sizable. Some of the members had begun talking about having a building campaign. At that time the price of land was rising at a rapid pace. Since interest rates were rather low, it was better to invest money in land than to have it sitting in the bank. Our treasurer, who was an astute businesswoman, found we could buy a small piece of land in a new development quite a few miles out in the country. We didn't think it would be suitable for a church, but we would be able to trade it when we did find a good location. Our members went to look at available land several times. But we didn't find any place that seemed suitable for a church building. It would be a distinct disadvantage if we had to build in a place far from our present location. Although adult members might get on a bus and come, the children would not be likely to follow our church school to a place that far away.

While we had been looking for a suitable location, I had in mind a sizable piece of land. I was thinking in terms of a place where there would be room for church school classes, a social hall, etc. But most of our members thought we should build something even if it was small. In Japan people tend to think of a building that will last about 25 years or so. Then it might be rebuilt, as their buildings are very easily torn down.

Our treasurer arranged to have the contractor sell the small parcel of land we had bought in the development, and then build our new church after tearing down the old shop. It was a long narrow piece of land with neighbors' houses right up against it on both sides. One Sunday she invited the contractor to meet with us after church to plan the kind of building we wanted. To my amazement they had mapped out the floor plan within an hour or so. I couldn't help recalling the full semester course at Hartford Seminary when we had to plan the educational wing of a church building!

Since the space was so narrow, we decided to have a "tatami" style floor as we had become used to that in our upstairs house church. We thought it would be more of an all-purpose room without chairs to be moved around when we had classes or a dinner. It was decided to have the parsonage upstairs and the sanctuary on the first floor. Since it was on a slope, there would be room for two or three cars under the building. It was right on the old bus road which made it very convenient for people to get there. But it was a noisy place with lots of traffic. We agreed to place the pulpit by the wall which was the farthest from the street in order to find the least noisy part. The toilet would be placed to the right of the entryway. The small kitchen would be just beyond that, with a small glassed-in "cry room" for mothers and babies in front of that. I had never seen one of those in any Japanese church, but the builder said it would be possible when I suggested it. We had quite a few noisy babies, and some of those without children welcomed the idea of a space where mothers could hear everything by means of a speaker, but they would be behind soundproof glass. So the rest of us could not hear the babies. This small room turned out to be very useful for small classes during the week, so that we did not need to heat the whole place.

We decided to have an old-fashioned toilet, as there was no space for a septic tank. We did have a system in my upstairs apartment where a tank provided some kind of chemical which could flush it without using much water. It was something like those used on airplanes. But there was still the need for periodic trips by the vacuum truck to take away the contents. Since the storage pit was much bigger and deeper in the ground, there was not so much of an odor, and the truck didn't come so often.

The first step in our financial campaign was to ask each member to pledge an amount to be given over a period of five years. We also applied to our denominational headquarters in Tokyo to get a low interest loan from their revolving fund. Our treasurer did all that paper work, and she managed to get it there by the deadline. Pastor Fujita, our district evangelism chairman, was on that committee and he promised to put in a good word for us. We were all very happy when we were granted the loan. We received another loan from a local bank. The method used by Japanese churches is to ask all the members to place their savings accounts in one bank, thus providing collateral for our loan. That was accomplished with no controversy, and everyone had enough faith in our ability to pay it back that they didn't seem to worry about losing their savings.

Another project suggested by Mrs. Fujikawa was to print a slim volume of my sermons and sell them for 500 yen or whatever donation people wished to give. Since I typed my Japanese sermons in Roman letters, that entailed a lot of work for her to transpose them to Japanese characters. When they printed a second pamphlet later, they taped the sermons each Sunday. Then one of the members listened to it and wrote it out in Japanese characters. These were distributed to other churches and to whoever might be interested.

After the old building had been torn down, we took the church school children to the vacant lot and took their picture. It was hard for me to visualize a church in this narrow space. But it turned out to be much better than I could imagine. The work began in August. In such crowded quarters it was not surprising that we had run-ins with the neighbors on each side.

Originally this old building had been part of a whole block of houses sharing the same roof. Through the years each section had been sold to different owners. But the house just to the left of our church lot still shared a wall with the old shop. Our builder erected a corrugated metal wall when the old one was torn down. The neighbor thought he should get a better wall, even though that one seemed to be an improvement over the old one. That man was notoriously hard to get along with. He belonged to a small belligerent sect of Buddhists who were different from what might be called mainline Buddhists. He was frustrated because he did not feel he could get his complaints heard properly by talking to a foreigner. Fortunately Mrs. Harada, the charter member about whom I wrote earlier, was willing to be our troubleshooter. She was a good diplomat with a lot of experience in settling disputes when she had been president of the PTA in her town.

She had helped settle a conflict over a new school building some years earlier. She persuaded him he was getting a fair deal. We were all surprised and pleased when he came over to join us at the time of our cornerstone laying ceremony. A few of our members gathered within the shell of the building to sing hymns and offer prayers to bless our sanctuary. Later at the dedication, his wife attended the service and contributed an offering.

The neighbor on the other side was afraid we would cut off too much light from his one story house. However, when Mrs. Harada talked to him, he admitted his house had been built illegally and he really couldn't complain to the town officials. It had been built on the lot back of the house which was flush with the bus road. That lot was zoned for only one building. Actually there was not a street with access to his house except the narrow space between our church and the house at the front of the lot. Evidently he had used bribery or some means to have the officials look the other way when his house was being built. As it turned out, our building did not cut off light as much as we feared it might.

Although there were long periods of time when we saw no workers at the building place, **as** the deadline drew near, they were working frantically even using lights at night. It reminded me of the way I usually worked on my term papers at graduate school. On the night before we were to move in, a workman was there all night painting the front of the building. We had enlisted members of our adult English classes as well as church members to help us on moving day which was to be on Sunday after church. Because the new church was so close, we needed only a small cart called a "rear car" to transport my furniture. It was a symphony of movement to see all those people carrying boxes and furniture from the old building to the new one. Since I had not had enough time to clear out everything, I discovered they had brought every item in sight, even tin cans containing old nails. But later that night I discovered the toilet paper was nowhere to be found! And someone had thrown away the nice evergreen branches I had obtained from the college for our Christmas decorations and had stored just behind my house. (We moved early in December).

In the hectic rush, I had not thought of the need to provide refreshments. But one of the neighbors whose children were in our church school, arrived with a tray of delicious cupcakes for a welcome snack when we took time to sit down for a cup of tea. Our women's group had been a great help in packing up dishes and books and small items before we moved. They also came back on Monday to help with the unpacking.

We all rejoiced at being in our new building at last. It was great for me to have my own space upstairs with my own kitchen which I no longer shared with the church. But everyone agreed there had been one big mistake. The builder had made the bathroom too small to be practical. I found it hard to get the door shut and then squeeze myself into the space where I did the preliminary washing up. Some of the members who had been watching the building going up had tried to warn me about the bathroom being too small. But I didn't actually take it in until I tried to use it. It seems the contractor thought a kitchen was more important to a foreigner than the bath. So he had made a rather large kitchen. Naturally I wanted the house to be usable for a Japanese minister who would follow me. It might be a family who would find the tiny bathroom very inconvenient.

One of my Jo Gakuin students who had graduated from a good technical college had become an architect who married an architect husband. She had always said she hoped she could help to plan our church, as she had taken part in our adult English classes in the house church, as well as the Sunday morning Bible class. One of my regrets was that I had not had the courage to suggest to our church members that they hire her as an architect instead of allowing our contractor to plan the building himself. I was afraid the members would think we could not afford that in our limited budget. But as it turned out, probably it would have been more economical in the long run.

Although our treasurer's husband was not a church member (he did become a Christian a few years later), he was very helpful in figuring out a solution. They could make the kitchen smaller and add that space to the bathroom. When we talked it over with the company, they agreed that the builder was partly to blame, and we were partly to blame for not monitoring it more carefully. They came to an agreement as to how we would divide the cost. We decided to do it right away and get it over. So from December until New Years, I couldn't use my kitchen stove or my bath. I could use the gas range downstairs in the church kitchen. And one of our church members who lived nearby urged me to use their bath as often as I wished.

Since Japanese workmen work mightily to finish everything by New Year's day, we knew they would do it quickly. On Christmas Eve while we were having our candle light service in the church downstairs, one workman was keeping lonely vigil upstairs in the bathroom where he had to monitor the oil stove placed there to hurry the drying process. For the first time I realized how much work is involved in making the bathroom floor truly waterproof. They put some kind of tar insulation between the tiles and the floor underneath. I felt sorry for the workman who had to spend Christmas Eve in such a way. But I knew that for him Christmas was just another day. I did take him some tea and Christmas cookies which he seemed to appreciate.

Before the renovation took place, we had our dedication service to which people of all the Kyodan churches in the city were invited. I still remember my feelings on the night before the big ceremony. It was a mixture of rejoicing in our accomplishment and amazement that this small group of Christians had been able to bring it about. I was able to share my joy with my close friend, Frances Bray, one of our Sunday nightclub members from my college days, who was then in Kobe. I invited her to represent my family and her father, Mr. Hutchison, the minister who had been such an important influence in my youth.

Many of our non-Christian neighbors also attended. Even though it is a strong traditional Buddhist village, many of the neighbors seemed to think our smart looking little building was an improvement in their town, and they wanted to celebrate with us. Of course many of the parents of our church school children who were not church members, came to the ceremony. We had about 100 people crowded into that small sanctuary that day.

We invited Pastor Fujita who had moved to another city by that time, to preach the sermon. Although he couldn't get there in time to give the sermon, he gave some remarks. He mentioned how he had tried to discourage me from starting the project unless I could finish it, and he seemed glad we had actually put up a building. The pastor who had succeeded him at the Ushita Church preached the sermon. He reminded us that the first Christian church in Europe recorded in Paul's letters, met at the home of Lydia, a woman who was a seller of purple. I was pleased when he mentioned that our church had contributed to the various social projects in our district even while we were still struggling to become a full blown church. Whenever our women had a bazaar, they always contributed some of the profit to the nursing home built by Kyodan churches in a nearby suburb for atom bomb victims, or the housing project for handicapped people in our district.

I was able to enjoy about four years living in the new parsonage where I had my own space. I still shared my upstairs bedroom as a church school class on Saturday afternoons. But we had room for all our English classes downstairs. Within two years we had the debt to the bank and to the denomination paid off. Members continued their special pledges in order to build up a fund to pay the new minister's full salary. I had been receiving a salary from the mission board. But during the last few years the church paid the house rent, my car expenses and my secretarial and utilities cost. They had also sent money to the joint fund in Tokyo to help pay for missionaries after the "oil shock."

By the time I retired in 1981, they had called a Japanese woman pastor to take my place. They did not have to ask the other churches for a subsidy, as they could be self-supporting by that time. Within a few years they notified me they were being recognized as a full-fledged church, and no longer just a preaching point. I found it rewarding to attend the 20th anniversary in 1986, the same year as the centennial of Hiroshima Jo Gakuin. The church asked me to preach the sermon on that occasion. We had a wonderful reunion with old and new members. Many of the young people from my English classes and my Bible classes made a special effort to attend.

I still correspond with many of the church people and those in my English classes. The minister has sent me the church bulletins periodically to help me keep up with the news. In spite of all the things I wish I could have done better, there is a church in Furuichi where there was none before. The fifteen years I spent in that village enriched my life and helped me to appreciate people in another culture. Although I embarked on the project without quite knowing where it would lead, by the grace of God we were able to gather a group of dedicated people to work with me to help this church to be born. This has confirmed my belief that when we take a leap of faith, we will be given the strength to do what seemed to be impossible.

PHOTOGRAPH SECTION

Doris Hartman in front of the House Church

Rev. Tatsuo Fujikawa and Doris conducting a
service in the House Church

Front view of new church

Doris teaching an English song.

Baptizing a baby

Doris and her successor Rev. Sadako Takase

Children's Memorial at Peace Park

Atomic Dome Memorial

<u>Children's Memorial</u> - A statue in the Peace Park in memory of Sadako, a girl who survived the atom bomb as a baby, but developed leukemia when she was 12. Her friends told her that if she folded one thousand paper cranes, it would bring her good luck. While she was in the hospital, her friends brought her origami paper and she devoted herself to folding paper cranes every day. Her younger brother strung them up above her hospital bed. Even though she got weaker and weaker, she still had hope that if she could fold 1000 cranes, she would get well.

When she had folded about 600 cranes, she died, and her classmates decided to finish 1000 cranes to place on her coffin. All the children took up an offering in order to build this (picture on prior page). It shows a child holding a folded crane aloft as a plea to the world never to allow children to experience an atomic bomb again.

The folded cranes have become a symbol of peace. Children from many countries make leis of folded cranes and bring them to hang at the foot of this statue.

<u>Atom Dome Memorial</u> - The people of Hiroshima have preserved this one ruin known as the atomic dome to remind the world of their hope that there will be "no more Hiroshimas."

GLOSSARY

GLOSSARY

Anata	Familiar form for <u>you</u>; term a wife uses for her husband.
Aisatsu	Formal greetings when meeting someone; or at the start of a meeting.
Bata-bata	Name used for 3 wheeled taxi used in early post-war years.
Booru	Ball when speaking of baseball.
Daikon	Long white radish with mild taste.
Fauru	Foul when used to speak of foul ball.
Fumie	Medal bearing the image of the virgin Mary which early Catholics stepped on to renounce their faith.
Furoshiki	Square piece of cloth used to carry things.
Futon	Bedding used for sleeping on tatami floor.
Gaijin	Used for non-Japanese people; literally <u>outside person</u>.
Geta	Wooden clogs used when walking on wet pavement or in a garden.
Gozaimasu	Polite form of the verb <u>to be</u>.
Hibachi	Ceramic pot filled with sand on which burning charcoal is laid to provide warmth for one's hands.
Hibakusha	Survivors of the atom bomb.
Higashi	East.
Hiragana	Adaptation of Japanese characters into a phonetic alphabet.
Hoocho	Special long sharp knife used by chefs as well as housewives.
Jinrikisha	Two wheeled cart pulled by a human being and later by bicycle; an early form of transportation.

GLOSSARY

J-3's	Short term missionaries who went to Japan to teach English for 3 years.
Jo Gakuin	Girls' school.
Kabuki	Japanese drama; combination of dance and drama with elaborate costumes.
Kana	Phonetic alphabet adapted from Japanese characters.
Kanai	The word for wife used by her husband.
Kanji	Japanese characters.
Katakana	Special phonetic alphabet used for foreign words.
Kiyoshi	Humble form for teacher.
Kyarameru	Caramel; Japanized form.
Kyodan	Union of Protestant churches formed at the end of World War II.
Meiji	Period in Japanese history near the end of the 19th century; time when power shifted from the feudal lords to the Emperor.
Miso	Bean paste used in soup and for flavoring.
Mochi	Glutinous rice; special food at New Years.
Nagarekawa	A church in Hiroshima.
Nishi	West.
Obento	Lunch box packed with rice and bits of meat, fish and vegetables.
Ofuro	Japanese bath.
Ohaiyo	Good morning.
Okusan	Polite word for wife used by those outside her family.
Omiyage	Presents brought home from a trip; gift to hostess.
Osushi	Rice mixed with sugar and vinegar made into balls with various toppings.

GLOSSARY

Rajio	Radio.
Ronin	Originally a samurai without a feudal lord now used for a student who failed the college entrance exam and takes a year off to prepare for the next year's exam.
Romaji	Japanese words written in the Roman alphabet.
Sensei	Literally, one born before; used after the name of teachers, doctors, and other leaders.
Shichirin	Clay pot used for cooking.
Shogun	Feudal lord.
Sushi	See "osushi," word without honorific $\underline{o}$.
Sukiyaki	Winter dish of beef and vegetables cooked at the table.
Sutoraiku	Japanized pronunciation for strike.
Tatami	Woven matting flooring.
Terebi	Japanized word for television.
Tofu	Food made of crushed soy beans.
Tokonoma	Alcove in the guest room with scroll and flower arrangement.
Tokugawa	Name of feudal lords who kept Japan isolated for 200 years before the Meiji era.
Wakarimasen	"I don't understand."
Yukata	Cotton summer kimono.
Yutampo	Metal hot water bottle.